The
Txtr's
A–Z

The
Txtr's
A–Z

compiled
and edited by
Andrew John
with **Stephen Blake**

Michael O'Mara Books Limited

First published in Great Britain in 2001 by
Michael O'Mara Books Limited
9 Lion Yard, Tremadoc Road
London SW4 7NQ

THIS EDITION SPECIALLY PRODUCED FOR WH SMITH 2001

Devised by David Crombie

A CIP catalogue record for this book is available
from the British Library

ISBN 1-85479-770-0

1 3 5 7 9 10 8 6 4 2

Designed and typeset by Martin Bristow

Printed and bound in Great Britain by Cox & Wyman,
Reading, Berks.

CONTENTS

INTRODUCTION

Shorter ways of saying things have been with us since speech began. 'Ug!' probably carried a multitude of meanings to a Neanderthal – and even today we hear it used by other people's kids.

It is argued that, because we live in a faster age, we need a faster language. The fastest way of communicating, of course, is the telephone, because speech is quick, but here we're concerned with the written and printed word, and that has become shorter with every change in communication.

Until recently, we found abbreviations mainly in specialized worlds such as science (EMR, for instance), the military (Sgt, Lt) and government (DfEE, MAFF). Many international organizations are known by their abbreviations (NATO, UNESCO), as are many charities (RSPCA, Oxfam, RSPB).

We also see the common abbreviations that we've used for years, such as RSVP at the bottom of an invitation and ways of saving money in contact ads by making four words into one when you want to describe an aspect of yourself (GSOH). Then there are the little expressions of affection that were (maybe still are) to be found written on the back of the envelope containing a love letter: SWALK, for instance, or HOLLAND. And of course we have all taken down notes while talking to someone on the telephone and written 'hd' for 'had', 'shd', for 'should', 'btw' for 'between' and so on.

Other abbreviations and acronyms have sprung up from social science, the media and everyday conversation. We don't think twice before speaking of a yuppie or a nimby these days, and often we find they're expressed entirely in lowercase letters, having earned their place in the popular lexicon.

Even in speech we use abbreviations without thinking about it. When we say 'Howdy?' we're saying 'How do you do?' Did 'Hi' come from 'Hiya', and that from 'How are you?'? Who knows? The ubiquitous 'gonna' is on everyone's lips, and, as a shortening of 'going to', is acceptable even in semiformal speech. And then there are the dozens of contractions such as 'we'd' for 'we would' or 'we had', and 'shouldn't' for 'should not'. These are not restricted to speech, of course, and are to be found in all but the most formal writing.

Some abbreviations, as we have seen, are acronyms. An acronym, strictly speaking, must spell a speakable word with its initials. DfEE doesn't count, but NATO does. While Oxfam isn't a set of initials as such, we can just about call it an acronym because elements of its full title, Oxford Committee for Famine Relief, are taken to form a sayable word.

So far, so good. We had a manageable language with many of its words conveniently shortened so that we could communicate more quickly. We all felt rather comfortable with that. Then came the revolution: email, WAP and text messages. Suddenly we find there's an abbreviation for just about anything – not to mention emoticons, but more on those later. Who would have thought – back in those balmy days of having just enough abbreviations to see you through an average day – that you would be able to say, lovingly, to the object of your desire, '**GtOutaMyDrms&In2MyLif**'? Or that, given a little more familiarity with the desired object, you would be saying, '**HABABWan2GtLcky?**'?

People are doing it all the time.

The beauty of the text message is that it's cheaper than a phone call and it makes it impossible to waffle: because you just don't have the space. What is even better is the way in which ingenious abbreviations have been contrived by text-messagers all over the world to capture a vaguely philosophical thought, a loving sentiment or a beautifully crafted obscenity. Text-messaging is nothing short of a phenomenon, and millions of them per day are crossing streets and crossing continents, some of them merely saying we'll meet up at seven o'clock, others exchanging important business information.

Certain conventions have established themselves as this way of sending brief messages via computer and mobile phone has evolved. You find in many abbreviations that a capital letter will represent a longer vowel sound, while the lowercase letter would represent a shorter one. '**LOks**' represents 'looks', for instance, in '**TOnlyThngThtLOksGOdOnMeIsU**', just as '**GOd**' reads 'good'. Not all are as complicated.

Emoticons (that's in the A–Z, too) are another matter altogether. With these cheeky, almost cryptogrammatical ciphers all sorts of messages are conveyed. They might look oddly at you down at the chippy if you presented them with a note saying you wanted **>->‹)))">&{{{{{{** but you could tell your mate on his WAP phone that this is what you're eating at the moment. So you needn't feel a **<:-(** or even have cause to say **<=** if someone sends you a string of characters from a computer keyboard. You should find the solution in our special section on emoticons. If not, it's because a new one's been invented since I wrote this.

So, as you browse through this comprehensive dictionary of text-messaging abbreviations, acronyms and emoticons, you'll be fascinated, titillated, educated and occasionally bewildered. What you won't be is bored. In fact, it's **UTU**, but, if you're **U4IT** you'll be **UAN** and will have **TTOYaL**.

Who knows? **ATEOTD** (or even **@TEOTD**), writing like this may one day take over completely. (Pitman's shorthand, **EtYa<30ut**.) Then we'll have to bring out a dictionary for people who like to use long words.

I could not have compiled this collection without the indefatigable help of Stephen Blake, who has taken on much of the donkey work and has sought out some of the more obscure and amusing examples.

As far as we've both been able to tell (and they're being invented all the time), the abbreviations in this dictionary are all **U2TM**, so, after studying them for a while, no one can say of you, '**YaLiftDsntREchTTopFl0r**'. **HAND**.

Andrew John
West Wales, February 2000

SYMBOLS AND FIGURES

#10	Number Ten Downing Street
%ge	percentage
&AT	and all that
&ILuvUSo	and I love you so
@ATOTDON	at all times of the day or night
@S1EX	at someone else's expense
@TEOTD	at the end of the day
0CnStpUNow	nothing can stop you now
0LeSThnBrL	nothing less than brilliant
0VOG	nothing ventured, nothing gained
1/2msre	half measure
1@AT	one at a time
1A=	first among equals
1C	first class
1DA@ATIm	one day at a time
1LOD	first line of defence
1nc	once
1OTD	one of these days
1sNE	one's never enough
1st2K	first to know
1stly	firstly
1StpAwA	one step away
1StpClosa	one step closer
1sty	firsty (thirsty)

1Wld	First World
1WW	First World War
1C1S	first come, first served
2	to, too, two
2B	to be
2BA	to be announced
2BC	to be continued/confirmed
2BON2BTITQ	to be or not to be, that is the question
2BR	to be resolved
2C	second class
2dAsYaLkEDA	today's your lucky day
2day	today
2Fw	too few
2Fw2Lte	too few, too late
2G2TA	too good to throw away
2G2W	too good to waste
2gthr4evr	together for ever
2gthr4evr&evr	together for ever and ever
2gthrWeRButiful	
	together we are beautiful
2Hot2Hndl	too hot to handle
2L8	too late
2L8	too late
2Lte	too late
2Mch	too much
2MCSTB	too many cooks spoil the broth
2Mny	too many

2moro	tomorrow
2nite	tonight
2Oftn	too often
2Son	too soon
2SW	to start with
2tyST	twentysomething
2tySTs	twentysomethings
2wcr	twicer
2WW	Second World War
2Erly	too early
2Mch2Ltle2LAt	too much, too little, too late
2WUA*	to wish upon a star
3C	third class
3dom	freedom
3LA	three-letter acronym
3sm	threesome
3sum	threesome
3tyST	thirtysomething
3tySTs	thirtysomethings
3Wld	third world
24/7	twenty-four hours a day, seven days a week
4	for, four
4AM	for a moment/minute
4BOW	for better or worse
4ce	force
4COL	for crying out loud
4fit	forfeit

4GOd	for good
4grnd	foreground
4GS	for goodness'/God's sake
4gt	forget/forgot
4gtIt	forget it
4gtn	forgotten
4LA	four-letter acronym
4LW	four-letter word
4m	form
4NK8	fornicate
4NK8r	fornicator
4play	foreplay
4ST	for some time
4sum	foursome
4t	fort, fought
4TGr8rGOd	for the greater good
4tnite	fortnight
4tune	fortune
4tyST	fortysomething
4tySTs	fortysomethings
4WD	four-wheel-drive
4x4	four-by-four (vehicle)
4evr	forever/for ever
4evr+2	forever and ever
4evrInLuv	forever in love
4evrKndOfLuv	forever kind of love
4EVRURS	forever yours

4EVRYRS	forever yours
5tyST	fiftysomething
5tySTs	fiftysomethings
6tyST	sixtysomething
6tySTs	sixtysomethings
7tyST	seventysomething
7tySTs	seventysomethings
8	ate
8tyST	eightysomething
8tySTs	eightysomethings
8–L8	eight till late
9tyST	ninetysomething
9tySTs	ninetysomethings
9!	no, no way
10Q	thank you
10X	thanks
12?	(do you) want to?
12M	one too many
100HST	onehundredsomething
100HSTs	onehundredsomethings
100ST	onehundredsomething
100STs	onehundredsomethings
102T12	ten to the dozen

A–Z OF TEXT MESSAGES

A

A ampere

Å angstrom

A2A aim(ing) to avoid

A2EIn2 able to enter into

A&A acronyms and abbreviations; again and again

A@A aimed at avoiding

AAA screaming

AAAIC as able as I can

AAB all-to-all broadcast

AAby as amended by

A@AC avoid(ing) at all costs

AAF avoid a Florida (as in US election)

AAM air-to-air missile; as a matter of fact

AAMOF as a matter of fact

AAO all aspects of

AAR against all risks

AAT and all that; average access time

AATR always at the ready

AATY after all these years

AB able-bodied seaman; *Artium Baccalaureus* (Bachelor of Arts, US); ah bless!; ample bosom

A&B	above and beyond
ABATS	Automatic Bit Access Test System
Abbr	abbreviated
Abbrv	abbreviated
ABCA	America Britain Canada Australia
ABEL	Advanced Boolean Expression Language
AbFab	absolutely fabulous; *Absolutely Fabulous*
ABH	actual bodily harm
ABIOS	advanced BIOS
ABIST	automatic built-in self-test (IBM)
ABLE	adaptive battery life extender
abr	abridge
ABR	automatic bit band rate detection; available bit rate
Abrd	abridged
Abs	absent, absence
ABSBH	Average Busy Season Busy Hour
AbsFab!	fabulous abdominals!
Absl	absolute
Absly	absolutely
AbsntMndd	absentminded
ABSOLOM	Agreement By Sending Out Lots Of Memos
Abstr	abstract
ABT	abort
Abt	about
Abt2	about to
A&BTCOD	above and beyond the call of duty

AbtTrn about turn

Abv above

AC alternating current

a/c account

A/c2 account to

A/c4 account for

ACA a cut above

AC/a.c. alternating current

ACATR a cut above the rest

A/c account

ACD automatic call distribution

ACE access control encryption/entry; Adobe Certified Expert

Ack acknowledge

Ack-Ack anti-aircraft (AA, from phonetic 'ack' for 'A')

ACNtu8T+ accentuate the positive

ACO all clapped out

ACOfWelthNowSuRoundsUUDrawFrmThsCALUNEd
a sea of wealth now surrounds you you draw from this sea all you need

ACOMI a case of mistaken identity

ActYaAgeNtYaShuSIz
act your age, not your shoe size

ACU automatic calling unit

AD accidental(ly) damage(d); Anno Domini

A–D analogue-to-digital

ADA Automatic Data Acquisitions (Programming Language named after Augusta Ada Lovelace)

ADABAS Adaptable Database System

ADC adaptive data compression (protocol) (Hayes); add with carry; aide-de-camp; analog to digital converter

ADCert a dead cert (certainty)

Adctd2Luv addicted to love

ADD Automatic Document Detection (WordPerfect)

Addn addition

Addnl additional(ly)

ADF automatic document feeder; automatically defined function

Adj adjacent

Adj2 adjacent to

Adm administration; Admiralty

ADN any day now

ADO active data objects

ADQ a direct question . . .

ADR address (computers); alternate dispute resolution

Adrd&Xplrd adored and explored

AdrnlnRsh adrenalin rush

ADSOS approved discretionary share option scheme

ADST approved deferred share trust

ADT	Atlantic Daylight Time
ADU	automatic dialling unit
AE	above or equal; actively encourage(d)/engage(d)
A&E	accident and emergency (casualty department in a hospital)
AEAABC	as easy as ABC
AEB	analog expansion bus
AF	*Archers* fanatic; audio frequency
AFAIA	as far as I'm aware
AFAIC	as far as I'm concerned
AFAICC	as far as I can see
AFAICS	as far as I can see
AFAIK	as far as I know/I'm concerned
AFAIP	as far as is possible
AFAIUI	as far as I understand/understood it
AFAP	as far as possible
AFB	air force base
AFctnt	affectionate
AFctntly	affectionately
AFEmAl	alpha female
AFK	away from keyboard
AFTP	anonymous file transfer protocol
Aftr	after
Aftrn0n	afternoon
AGM	annual general meeting

AGoNaBmpNoMorW/NoBgFatWmn

	ain't gonna bump no more with no big fat woman
AgrEmnt	agreement
Agt	agent
AGT	all good things
AGTWHBA	a good time was had by all
AGW	actual gross weight
AHAP	as humanly as possible
AhB!	Ahhh, Bisto!
Ahd	ahead
AHzBEn	a has-been
AI	analog input; artificial intelligence
AI!	as if . . .!
AIAGDW	all in a good days work
AIAS	as I've always said
AICI	as I see it
AID	artificial insemination by donor
AIFF	Audio Interchange File Format
AIH	artificial insemination by husband
AINFOT	all in the fullness of time
AintOLkeIt	ain't nothing like it
AintOLkeTRThngBAB	
	ain't nothing like the real thing, baby
AintNoMntnHiEnuf2KEpMeFrmU	
	ain't no mountain high enough to keep me from you

AintNoStPinUNow

        aint no stopping you now

AISB as I said before

AITM all in the mind

AIW as it were/was

AJA all joking apart

AjAint0BtaNo age ain't nothing but a number

AJU all jacked up

AKA also known as

AL2gthr altogether

Alc alcohol(ic)

ALCM air-launched cruise missile

ALGOL algorithmic oriented language

ALGTCTAE all good things come to an end

ALGTMCTAE all good things must come to an end

ALIHve2DoIsDrm

        all I have to do is dream

ALIkUMEnIt act like you mean it

Aliph aliphatic

ALIWanIsU all I want is you

Alk alkaline

Alky alkalinity

ALLIADT a little learning is a dangerous thing

ALMth&Trsrs all mouth and trousers

ALNiteLng all night long

ALOr0 all or nothing

ALOvaNow all over now

ALP$&Wnd all piss and wind
ALrIt all right/alright
Alt alternate; alteration
ALThosCrvs&MeWivNoBrks
　　　　　　all those curves and me with no brakes
ALTImHI all time high
ALtleLuv? a little love?
ALTLuvInTWrld all the love in the world
ALU arithmetic and logic unit
ALwAsL0kOnTBrItSIdOfLIf
　　　　　　always look on the bright side of life
Alwys always
Alwys&4evr always and for ever
a.m. ante meridiem (before noon)
AM4I! always mad for it
AMA against medical advice
AMAl alpha male
AMAP as much/many as possible
AME a moving experience
AmEx American Express
AML all my love
AMLUV all my love
AMOmntOnTLpsIsALIfTImOnTHips
　　　　　　a moment on the lips is a lifetime on the hips
Amt amount
AN above named; in the year . . .
Anal analysis, analytical(ly)

&	and
&Sum	and some
AnE	any
AnE1OutThre?	anyone out there?
AnENEWS4Me?	have you got any news/information/gossip for me
ANI	automatic number identification
Anon	anonymous
AnothaDAInParadIs	
	another day in paradise
Anrk	anorak
Ans	answer
ANS	autonomic nervous system
AO	analogue output; atomic orbital
AO2	as opposed to
AOB	any other business
AOBTS	all over bar the shouting
AOC	age of consent
AOD	areas of doubt
AO/DI	always on/Dynamic ISDN
AOL	all our love;
AOLUV	all our love
AOM	age of majority
AONB	area of outstanding natural beauty
AOQL	average outgoing quality level
AOR	any old rubbish
AOS	add or subtract

AOTWR	another off-the-wall remark
A/P	accounts payable
APB	all-points bulletin;
API	application program interface
App	apparatus
APPI	advanced peer-to-peer internetworking
Approx	approximate(ly)
Approxn	approximation
APrx	approx (approximately)
Apt	apartment
APt	appointment
APW	augmented plane wave
Aq	aqueous
AQL	acceptable quality level
AR	ample room;
A/R	accounts receivable
ARE	acronym-rich environment
Arhed	airhead
ArmCndE	arm candy
ARngmnt	arrangement
Arom	aromatic
ARORL	a representation of real life
Artcl	article
ARU	audio response unit
ARU&NP2G	all revved up and no place to go
ARve	arrive
AS	absolutely superb

A/S	advanced/supplementary
ASAHP	as soon as humanly possible
ASAP	as soon as possible; automatic switching and processing
ASC	a successful conclusion
AsFa	as far
A$Kkr	ass kicker
ASL	above sea level
A/S/L	Age/Sex/Language or Age/Sex/Location
ASM	air-to-surface missile
ASmbl	assemble
ASmblPt	assembly point
ASn	association
ASOHD	a sense-of-humour deficit
ASOHTP	a sense-of-humour transplant
ASP	active server pages
Assoc	associate
Assocd	associated
Assocg	associating
Assocn	association
AsSumbdy1nceSEd . . . &IQuot	as somebody once said . . . and I quote
ASt	assistant
A$W	asswipe
asym	asymmetric(al)(ly)
AT	any time
at	atomic

@	at
AT11Hr	at the eleventh hour
ATA	achieve that aim
ATB	all the best
ATC	average total cost
ATD	actual time of departure
ATDONite	at the dead of night
ATE	after the event
ATEOEE	at the expense of everything else
ATEOTD	at the end of the day
AthAT	authoritarian attitude
ATHHB	after the horse has bolted
ATKEM&Ms	at the keyboard eating M&Ms
AtLEstIDntHavAFAcLIkaBmusdHaDck	
	at least I don't have face like a bemused haddock
ATLT	all the latest technology
ATM	at the moment
Atm	atmosphere; atmospheric
ATM	automated teller machine (cash point)
ATM-DXI	asynchronous transfer mode-data exchange interface
ATN	any time now
ATOU	always thinking of you
ATR	at the ready
A@TR	always at the ready
ATS	always the same

@T11Hr	at the eleventh hour
@TDONite	at the dead of night
@TEOEE	at the expense of everything else
@TEOTD	at the end of the day
Attn	attention
@TR	at the ready
ATUL	any time you like
ATWT&BA	all the way there and back again
ATYL	any time you like
AU	audio (as stored computer data); astronomical unit
AUDIX	Audio Information Exchange
AUT?	are you there?
Aux	auxiliary
Av	average
Ave	avenue
Avg	average
AVR	automatic voice recognition
AVT	applied voice technology
AWA	as well as
AWHFY?	are we having fun yet?
AWOE	a wealth of experience
AWOL	all walks of life; absent without leave
AX	architecture extended; automatic transmission

B

B	be
B13	baker's dozen
B24N	bye-bye for now
B2B	back to basics; back-to-back
B2B	business-to-business
B2E	business to employees
B2F	back to front
B2S	born to serve
B4N	bye for now
B5	*Babylon 5*
BA	best available; Bachelor of Arts; bad apple
BA&F	budget, accounting and finance
BAB	baby
B&B	bed & breakfast
BABBluii	baby blue eyes
BABDoL	baby doll
BABIDntCAr	baby I don't care
BABItsU	baby, it's you
BABs	babies
BABUCnDrIvMyCa	
	baby you can drive my car
BABx2	baby, baby
BAC?	by any chance?
BAFO	best and final offer

BAK	back at keyboard; Binary Adaption Kit (Microsoft)
Bak2YaR0ts	back to your roots
Bal	balance
BAL	basic assembly language; blood alcohol level
BALUN	balanced to unbalanced
BANANA	Build Absolutely Nothing Anywhere Near Anyone
BARF	Best Available Retrofit Facility
BASM	built-in assembler
BATB	begin at the beginning
B@TM	busy at the moment
BATNEEC	best available techniques not entailing excessive costs
BAU	business as usual
BB	big boy; best of breed; bulletin board
B&B	bed and breakfast
BB4N	bye-bye for now
BBA	balanced budget amendment
BBB	bed, breakfast, bath
BBC	British Broadcasting Corporation
BBFN	bye-bye for now
BBIAB	be back in a bit
BBL	be back later
BBQ	barbecue
BBS	be back soon; bulletin board system
BBSD	be back soon, darling

BC	before Christ
BCC	blind carbon copy; blocked call cleared
BCD	Bad Conduct Discharge
BCNU	be seeing you
BCOS	best chance of success
BCP	binary communications protocol
BCU	big close-up
BCWP	budgeted cost of work performed
BCWS	budgeted cost of work scheduled
BD	Bachelor of Divinity; by definition
BD!	big deal!
BDA	battle damage assessment; bomb damage assessment
BdBy	bad boy
BDOS	basic disk operating system
BDSM	bondage and domination, sadomasochism
BE	back entrance; below or equal; bill of exchange
B&E	breaking and entering
BEAV	binary editor and viewer
BEG	big evil grin
BELT	bacon egg lettuce and tomato sandwich
BER	basic encoding rules; bit error rate
BERT	bit error rate test/tester
BEst	beast
BeTaLuvNxtTIm	better love next time

BEV	Black English Vernacular
BF	boyfriend; brought forward
B/F	background/foreground
BFC	bare-faced cheek
.BFC	Briefcase (file name extension) (Microsoft)
BFN	bye for now
BFOL	brutal fact(s) of life
BFrEWivYa<3	be free with your heart
BG!	big grin!
BGM	background music
BGOd2YaSlf	be good to yourself
BGr	bagger
BGT	business growth training
BGWM	be gentle with me (please)
BH	bounty hunter
BHaP	be happy
BHD	bad hair day
Bhnd	behind
bhp	brake horsepower
BI	background information; bibliographic instruction; binary input
Bi	bisexual
BIB	biggest is best; black is black
BIC	best in class
BICBW	but I could be wrong
BID	two times a day (medical)
BiDi	bi-directional

BildrsBm	builder's bum
Bin	been
.BIN	binary (file name extension)
BINAC	binary automatic computer
BINHEX	binary-hexadecimal
BION	believe it or not
BIOS	basic input/output system
BIOYI/OP	blow it out your I/O port
BISP	business information system program
BIST	built-in self-test
BItMe	bite me
BITW	best in the world
BiZniZ	business
BJC	bubble-jet colour (printer technology)
BK	big kiss
Bk	book
Bkfst	breakfast
Bkgrnd	background
BKOl	be cool
Bksp	backspace
BL	backlit
BL	belly laughing
BlaBlaBla	blah, blah, blah
BLNDE	blonde
BlOmn	blooming
BlOmnHec!	blooming heck!
BLT	bacon, lettuce and tomato (sandwich)

BMB0	bimbo
BmClEvj	bum cleavage
BMX	bicycle motocross
Bn	being
BN	binary number
BN2A	best/better not to ask
BnanaN0s	banana nose
B0	back order; body odour; black out; box office; binary output
B0ABB	best of a bad bunch
B0AF	birds of a feather
B0b	boob
B0B	booby; best of breed
B0E	back-of-the-envelope (calculations)
B0F	beginning of file
B0F	birds of a feather
B0FH	bastard operator from hell (may describe your system administrator)
B0G0F	buy one, get one free
BoLy	Bolly (champagne)
BoLyw0d	Bollywood
B0M	beginning of message
B0nhed	bonehead
B0P	balance of payments
Borin	boring
B0TEC	back-of-the-envelope calculation
B0V	best of variety

Boyf	boy friend
BOzBLE	booze belly
BP	beautiful people
BP	blood pressure; boiling point
bp	boiling point
BPD	barrels per day
BPFH	bastard programmer from hell
BPI	bits per inch; blocks per inch; bytes per inch
b.p.m.	beats per minute (music)
BPP	bits per pixel
BQ2H	best qualified to help
BRB	be right back
BRET	best result every time
BrLOhEd	brillohead
Brn2BMyBaB	born to be my baby
BrnBABBrn	burn, baby, burn
BrnW/A:-)OnYaFAc	
	born with a smile on your face
Bros	brothers
BRUS	boys are us
BS	backspace;
B/S	balance sheet
BSc	Bachelor of Science
Bscn	bit scan (computer)
BSE	bovine spongiform encephalopathy
BSOn	be soon
BST	British Summer Time

Bsy	Busy
Bt	Baronet
BT	bad timing; British Telecommunications
BT2YaSlf	be true to yourself
BTA	better than average; but then again
BTAICBW	but then again I could be wrong
BTAIM	be that as it may
BTB	by the bye
BTBUCB	be the best you can be
BTC	by the sea
BTDT	been there, done that
BTDTGTTS	been there, done that, got the t-shirt
BTF	balance to follow
BthD8	birth date
BthD8?	when were you born?
BtmFEdr	bottom feeder
BTR	bit test and reset
BTr1/2	bitter half (husband, wife, partner)
BTS	back to school;
BTTP	back to the point
Btw	between
BTW	by the way
BU!	bottoms up!
BuBle	bubble
BUKT	but you knew that
BURMA	be upstairs ready, my angel
BuThed	butthead

Butiful beautiful
BV book value
BVM Blessed Virgin Mary (on inscriptions and in epithets)
BVR beyond visual range
BW band width; best wishes; black and white
B&W black and white
BWC bandwidth compression; Beauty Without Cruelty
Bwd backward
BW\MIHM butter wouldn't melt in his/her mouth
BW\MITM butter wouldn't melt in their mouths
BWTHDID? but what the heck do I do . . . ?
BWTHDIDN? but what the heck do I do now . . . ?
BWTHDIK? but what the heck do I know . . . ?
BX big kiss; base exchange
Bx box
By busy
BYKT but you knew that
ByMEtsGrlSOWot? boy meets girl so what?
BYO bring your own
BYOB bring your own beer (or bottle or booze)
BYungBFOlshBHaPy
be young be foolish be happy

C

c	circa (approximately)
C	see
C	cannot/can't; could not/couldn't
C\GE	can't get enough
C\MIT	can't make it tonight
C4	Channel 4 (television)
C4D	call for discussion
C4M	care for me
C5	Channel 5 (television)
C/A	capital/credit/current account
CA!	chocks away!
cal	calorie
Calc	calculate
Calcd	calculated
Calcg	calculating
Calcn	calculation
CAM	computer-aided manufacture
CantWAt2XU	can't wait to kiss you
CATC!	count all the chads!
CATP	cat among the pigeons
CATV	cable televison; community antenna television (original name for cable TV)
CB	call back; citizen's band (radio)

CBA	can (or can't) be arsed (interchangeable, but usually in negative); cost–benefit analysis
CBD	cash before delivery
CBE	Commander (of the Order of the) British Empire
CBOH	clean bill of health
CCTV	closed-circuit television
CCW	counter clockwise
CD	compact disc
C&D	collection and delivery
CD-E	compact disc – erasable
CD+MIDI	CD-ROM that includes audio and MIDI data
CD-R	compact disc – recordable
CD-ROM	compact-disc read-only memory
CD-RW	compact disc – rewritable
CD-V	compact disc – video
CD-WO	compact disc – write once
CE	Common Era (alternative to AD)
CEG	continuous edge graphics
CEO	chief executive officer
Cert	certificate
CEST	Central Europe Summer Time
CET	Central Europe Time
CF	cash flow; cost and freight; cystic fibrosis
C&F	cost and freight
cf.	compare (Latin *confer*)
CFD	call for discussion

CFR	constant failure rate
CGA	colour graphics adapter
CGE	can't get enough
CGTSTD	can't get the staff these days
CHAR	character
CHC	cohabiting couple
.CHK	CHKDSK (file name extension)
CHOHW	come hell or high water
ChPn	chairperson
Chq	cheque
CHUR	see how you are
CHYA!	chill ya!
CIA	Central Intelligence Agency
CIH	cash in hand
CIIC	see if I care
CIO	cut it out
CKD	completely knocked down
CLAB	crying like a baby
Cld	could
Cld9	cloud 9
CldItBMgic?	could it be magic?
Clevr&GodL0kin!	
	clever and good looking !
CLnt	cell-net (phone)
.CLP	clipboard (file name extension) (Windows)
CLS	clear screen
CLT	clear the decks

cm	centimetre
CM	check mate;
CM?	c'est moi?
.CMD	command (file name extension)
CMF	creative music format
CMIIW	correct me if I'm wrong
CMLB	call me later, baby
CMY	cyan-magenta-yellow (colour model)
CMYK	cyan-magenta-yellow-black (colour model)
Cn	seeing
Cn	cannot/can't
CND	Campaign for Nuclear Disarmament
CNDO	complete neglect of differential overlap
Cngrtultns	congratulations
CnIFlrtWivU?	can I flirt with you?
CNS	central nervous system
Cnt23	count to three
CntGtEnufOfU	can't get enough of you
CntHlpFLnInLuvWivUALOvrAgn	
	can't help falling in love with you all over again
Co	company
CO	cuddle on
COAX	coaxial cable
COD	cash (collect in US) on delivery
coeff	coefficient
CofB	could have been
COkBOk	cook book

COl	cool
COL	cost of living
COlB!	Cool Britannia!
COLD	computer output to laser disk
COlTOl	cool tool
Com	commercial(ly)
.COM	command (file name extension); commercial business (domain name) (Internet)
COM1	first serial port (asynchronous port)
COM2	second serial port
COM3	third serial port
COM4	fourth serial port
COMM	communications
Compd	compound
Compn	composition
CON	console (includes Keyboard and Screen)
Conc	concentrate
Concd	concentrated
Concg	concentrating
Concn	concentration
COND	condition
Cond	conductivity
CONFIG	configuration
Const	constant
Contg	containing
CONTONE	continuous tone
Corrie	*Coronation Street*

COS	compatible operating system
COT	cuddle on tight(ly)
COTF	concentrate on the future
COTS	commercial off-the-shelf (software)
CP	chemically pure; Congregation of the Passion; copy protected
c.p.	candlepower
Cpl	Corporal
CPO	compulsory purchase order
CPR	cardiopulmonary resuscitation
CPS	characters per second; cycles per second
cps	cycles per second
CPU	central processing unit
CR	credit
CRAYON	create your own newspaper
CrEp	creep
crit	critical
Cr0l2BKInd	cruel to be kind
CRT	cathode-ray tube
CRUD	create, retrieve, update, delete
Crwl	crawl
Cryst	crystalline
Crystd	crystallized
Crystg	crystallizing
Crystn	crystallization
CS	chickenshoot
C/S	client/server

CSA	common sense advice
CSG	chuckle, snigger, grin
CSL	computer sensitive language
CSOS	cornerstone of society
CSThnknAU	can't stop thinking about you
CSU	channel service/switching unit
CTCP	client-to-client protocol
CTE	cost(ing) the Earth
CTRL	control
CTS	clear to send
CTT	capital transfer tax
CU	see you
CU@TGim	see you at the gym
CU2Nite@8YaPlce?	
	see you tonight at eight, your place?
CUA	see you again/around
CUC	called-up capital
Cud	could
CUD?	can you dance?
CUIC	see you in court
CUIMD	see you in my dreams
CUL	see you later
CUL8r	see you later
Cum	come
Cum2gthrRiteNow	
	come together right now
CUMIT?	can you make it tonight?

CUO	see you online
CUOnEzESt	see you on easy street
.CUR	cursor (file name extension)
CURA	cover your actions
CUS	see you soon
CUSTL8r	see you some time later
CUSTS	see you some time soon
CUT	see you there
CUTAH?	can't you take a hint?
CV	curriculum vitae; cultivar
CW	clockwise
C&W	country and western (music)
CW2CU	can't wait to see you
CW2CUL8R	can't wait to see you later!
CW2HU	can't wait to hold you
CWOT	complete waste of time
cwt	hundred weight
CWUAS	chat with you again soon
CWUL8r	chat with you later
CY	see you
CYA	see you
CYAMIT?	can you make it tonight?
CYD?	can you dance?
CYRS	cover yours
Cz	czar

D did not/didn't

D do not/don't

D4LA disenhanced four-letter acronym (that is, a TLA/3LA)

D8 date

DA2DA day to day, day-to-day

DAB digital audio broadcasting

DAC digital-to-analogue converter

DAD dispense as directed

DA day; definite article; delayed action; dollar account

D–A digital-to-analogue

DAPS direct-access programming system

DAr2BDFrnt dare to be different

DAS do a shop

DAT digital audio tape

DATACOM data communications

Datacom data communications

Datacor data correction

Datanet data network

Datap data transmission and processing

DAV digital audio-video

DAVB digital audio and video broadcasting

DAVIC Digital Audio-Visual Council

DB database; data buffer; device bay; dirtbag

dB decibel(s)

D\BAF don't be a fool

DBC death by chocolate

DBM database manager

DBME database management environment

DBMS data base management system

DBNO down but not out

DBS database server; direct-broadcast satellite; DOS boot record

D\BST don't be so tight

DBV digital broadcast video

DC debit card; Detective Constable; direct current

DCAM digital camera; direct chip attach module

DCD data-carrier detect

DCF discounted cash flow

DCI Detective Chief Inspector

DCM do call me

D\CM don't call me

DCMAT do call me any time

D&D death and destruction/decay; drunk and disorderly

DD? what's today's date?

DDD decisions, decisions, decisions

DDI digital data indicator

D\DITP don't dwell in the past

DdntIBloYaMndThsTme?
> didn't I blow your mind this time?

DdntWeGo2DfrtSchls?
> didn't we go to different schools?

DDO daily dose/digest of

DDP digital data processor

DdUHrtYaslfWenUFeLFrmHvn?
> did you hurt yourself when you fell from heaven?

Decomp decompose

Decompd decomposed

Decompg decomposing

Decompn decomposition

Defrag defragment

DEp deep

DEpr deeper

Deriv derivative

DES Data Encryption Standard

Det determine

Detd determined

Detg determining

Detn determination

DF damage free

DFDR digital flight data recorder

DFLA disenhanced four-letter acronym (that is, a TLA/3LA)

Dfnt definite

Dfntly	definitely
DG	director general
DGAWU	don't get all worked up
Dgbrth	dogbreath
DGMAAN	don't give me an answer now
DGT	don't go there
D\GTT2T	don't give them time to think
DGTT2T	don't give them time to think
DH	dickhead
DHE	data-handling equipment
DHTML	dynamic HTML
DI	Detective Inspector; different idea; do it; dying intestate
D&I	drunk and incapable
diam	diameter
DIDO	data input, data output
DIF	data interchange format
DIKU?	do I know you?
Dil	dilute
Dild	diluted
Dilg	diluting
Diln	dilution
DILY	darling, I love you
DIN	data identification number
DINKIES	(people with) dual income, no kids
DIP	Document Image Processing
Dir	director(y)

Dissoc dissociate
Dissocd dissociated
Dissocg dissociating
Dissocn dissociation
Distd distilled
Distg distilling
Distn distillation
DITYID? did I tell you I'm distressed?
DiVE divvy
DIY do-it-yourself
DJ disc jockey; desk jockey
DJ2C don't jump to conclusions
DK don't know
DKST don't keep saying that
DL damage limitation; data link; dead letter/link
dl decilitre(s)
DL download (also d/l)
DLD deadline date
DLG devilish little grin
DLitt Doctor of Letters (Latin, *Doctor Litterarum*)
DLL dynamic link library
DLM! don't lecture me!
DLS Data Link Switching (IBM)
DLTBBB don't let the bed bugs bite
DLTBGUD don't let the b'ds grind you down
DMI don't mention it; desktop management interface

DMP	design-making process
DMs	Doc Martens
DMTW	don't mention the war
DMY	day month year
DMZ	demilitarized zone
DNA	do/did not answer
DngBt	dingbat
DNIS	dialled number identification service
DNLA	Discovery of Natural Latent Ability
D-Note	500-dollar bill (US)
DNS	domain name server/system
DntArgu	don't argue
DntAsk	don't ask
DntBCrOlWenLuvTrnsBd	
	don't be cruel when love turns bad
DntBSq	don't be square
DntSht	don't shout
DntSwr	don't swear
DntUNoMeFrmSumwer	
	don't you know me from somewhere
do	ditto (the same)
DOA	dead on arrival; drunk on arrival
DOB	date of birth
DOD	date of death/disease
DoH	ditto (the same) here
Doin	doing
DoN	doing

DoNethngUWan2Do
>do anything you want to do

DOr door
DOS disk operating system
DoUACpt do you accept?
DoUAgrE? do you agree?
DoUCmHrOftn? do you come here often?
DoUEvnNoWotThtMEns?
>do you even know what that means?

DoUMndIfIFntsizAbtU?
>do you mind if I fantasize about you?

DoUMndIfIStrAtU4Amin?IWan2RmbrYaFce4MyDrms
>do you mind if I stare at you for a minute? I
>want to remember your face for my dreams.

DoUWan2ShgOrShldISaSry?
>do you want to shag or should I apologize

DoWotUDo2Me do what you do to me
DP data processing
DP! don't panic
DPOB date and place of birth
DPS dividends per share
DpStk dipstick
DPU data-processing unit
DQ drama queen
DQMOT don't quote me on this
DR debit; debt recovery; doctor
DR? Doctor Who

DRA	don't recognize acronym
DrGnMeDwn	dragging me down
Drk	dork
DrkbrAN	dorkbrain
Drln	darling
DrmaQEn	drama queen
DrmTDrm	dream the dream
Dr0g	droog (sidekick)
DrpM	drop 'em
DrwninInTCOLuv	
	drowning in the sea of love
DS	deeply suspect; Detective Sergeant
D&S	demand and supply
DSDD	double-sided, double-density (diskette)
DSE	data storage equipment
DSHD	double-sided, high-density (diskette)
DSN	Deep Space Network
DSOC	don't stand on ceremony
DSP	digital signal processing
DSQD	double-sided, quad-density (diskette)
DSR	data set ready
DST	daylight saving time; don't say that
DSTM	don't shoot the messenger
DT	daylight time
DTA	daily travel allowance;
DTB	data transfer bus
DTD	direct to disk (computer); dated

DTL	down the line
DTP	desk-top publishing
DTR	data terminal ready
DTRT	do the right thing
DTS	data-transmission system; don't think so
DTT@H	don't try this at home
DTTBaBOWTBW	
	don't throw the baby out with the bath water
DUC?	did you call?
DUCWIC?	do you see what I see?
DUHWIH?	do you hear what I hear?
DUK?	do you know . . . ?
DuL	dull
DUN	Dial-Up Networking (Microsoft)
DUT?	do you think . . . ?
DV	declared value; double vision; digital video
DVAOA	déjà vu all over again (as the Americans say)
DVB	digital video broadcast
DVC	desktop video conferencing; digital video camera
DVD	digital versatile disk
DVD-RAM	digital versatile disc-RAM
DVD-ROM	digital versatile disc-ROM
DVE	digital video effect
DvlInDsGIs	devil in disguise
DVM	digital volt meter

Dvors	divorce
DVR	digital video recorder
.DVR	Device Driver (file name extension)
DW4M	don't wait for me
DWBH!	don't worry, be happy!
DwEb	dweeb
DWI	driving while intoxicated
Dwn	down
DwnTme	downtime
Dx	Diagnosis
DXF	drawing exchange format
DXT	data extract facility
DYaOH	do your own homework
DZ	drop zone

E

E&E experience and expertise

E2EG ear-to-ear grin

E2TO each to their own

E3LA extended three-letter acronym (that is, an FLA/4LA) (EU)

EAK everyone already knows

EAROM electrically alterable read-only memory

eBkn e-banking

eBnk e-bank

eBOk e-book

eBOkn e-booking

eBOOK electronic book

EC European Community (now EU)

ECD enhanced color display; enhanced compact disc

ECG echocardiograph; electrocardiogram; electrocardiograph

eCmmrc e-commerce

ED effective dose

EDI electronic data interchange

EE *EastEnders*

EFIGS English, French, Italian, German, Spanish

EFL English as a foreign language

EG evil grin

EGA	enhanced graphics adapter
EGM	extraordinary general meeting
EGR2PLS	eager to please
EgrOp	egroup
EgrOps	egroups
EGS	everything goes slowly
EIE	enough is enough
EIIR	Queen Elizabeth II
EINE4U	enough is never enough for you
Ejit	eejit (idiot)
EK	everyone/everybody knows
ELS	entry level system
eLuv	e-love
e-Luvn	e-loving
eM	e-mail
EMFBI	excuse me for butting in
EMI	every man for 'imself
eMMe	e-mail me
EMOTICON	emotive icon
EMS	eat my shorts; everything moves slowly
ENO	English National Opera
ENT	ear, nose and throat
Enuf	enough
EO	equal opportunities
EOC	Equal Opportunities Commission
EOD	end of discussion
EOL	end of lecture

EOL	end of line
EOM	end of message
EOSP	employee share-ownership plan
EOT	end of thread (meaning: end of discussion)
EPS	Encapsulated Postscript
=FA	equality for all
Equil	equilibrium
Equiv	equivalent
ERR	Error
ERW	enhanced radiation weapon
Esc	escape
ESOTW	every stage/step of the way
ESP	extrasensory perception; especially
Estbd	established
ESTD	easier said than done
Estg	estimating
Estn	estimation
eSX	e-sex
ET	Eastern Time; extraterrestrial
ETD	estimated time of departure
ETDrnk&BMERE42moroUDiet	eat, drink and be merry for tomorrow you diet
EtTRch	eat the rich
ETUSGICAL	every time you say goodbye, I cry a little
EtYa<30ut	eat your heart out
EtYaslfHOl	eat yourself whole

EULA	end-user licence agreement
eV	electron volt
EV	ever ready
Evap	evaporate
Evapd	evaporated
Evapg	evaporating
Evapn	evaporation
EvlWmn	evil woman
EvrEbdEWans2BU	
	everybody wants to be you
EvrEbdEWansU	everybody wants you
EvrEBoDsL@U	everybody's laughing at you
EvrEDAInEvrEWA	
	every day in every way
EvrlstnLuv	everlasting love
EvrlstnLuv	everlasting love
EvrRdy	ever ready
Evry1AK	everyone already knows
Evry1K	everyone knows
EvryLtleThngUDoIsMgic	
	every little thing you do is magic
EvryMveUMkeILBWtchnU	
	every move you make I'll be watching you
EvryN&T	every now and then
EvryThgWLBALriteInTEnd	
	everything will be all right in the end
Evrythng	everything

Evrywhr	everywhere
EWE	every woman for 'erself
Examd	examined
Examg	examining
Exec	executive
EXPO	World Exposition
Expt	experiment
Exptl	experimental(ly)
Ext.	external; extract
Extd	extracted
Extg	extracting
Extn	extraction
EZ	easy
EzELIkSundAAM	
	easy like Sunday morning
EZEPZE	easy peasy

F

F2F face to face
F2K first to know
F2T free to talk (a statement of fact)
F2T? are you free to talk? (a question)
F4A free for all
FA fait accompli; Football Association
FAB OK (as in *Thunderbirds*); from all backgrounds
FAP file access protocol
FAQ frequently asked questions
FAT file allocation table
fave favourite
4n fawn
FAX facsimile
.FAX Fax (file name extension)
FBA Fellow of the British Academy
FBW! flash, bang, wallop!
FC football club
F&C fish and chips
FCFS first come, first served
FD floppy disk; floppy drive; full duplex
FDC floppy disk controller
FDI foreign direct investment
FDISK fixed disk

FDR	Franklin Delano Roosevelt (32nd President, USA)
FDROTFL	falling down rolling on the floor laughing
FDX	full duplex
FedEx	Federal Express
FEEA	Foreign Exchange Equalization Account
FEl	feel
FElFrE FElGOd	feel free, feel good
FElLuvCumnOn	feel love coming on
FElng	feeling
FEITNEdIM	feel the need in me
FEnd	fiend
FEP	front-end processor
FEPROM	flash EPROM
fermn	fermentation
FEVRYRS	forever yours
FF	fart-face
ff.	following pages/folios; fortissimo
FFB	fixed-fee basis
FFH	friend from hell
FFS	fast file system
FGS	for goodness'/God's sake
FICCL	frankly, I couldn't care less
FIFA	Fédération Internationale de Football Association
FIFO	first in, first out
FIL	first in line

FILO	first in, last out
FISH	first in, still here
FITB	fill in the blank
FITB(s)	fill in the blank(s)
FIX	Federal Internet Exchange
FKLW	finders keepers, losers weepers
FL	finishing line
FLA	four-letter acronym
Fld	field
FL&FF	footloose and fancy free
FLIinCulrs	flying colours
Fl0r	floor
.FLR	folder (file name extension)
FLT	forklift truck
FLW	famous last words
FM	family mediation; Field Marshal; frequency modulation
FMDIDGAD	frankly, my dear, I don't give a damn
FMTUEWTK	far more than you ever wanted to know
FNF	file not found
FngusFAC	fungus face
Fntastic!TlbsJstMlt	fantastic the pounds just melt
Fntsiz	fantasize
FO	Flying Officer; Foreign Office
FOAF	friend of a friend
f.o.b.	free on board

FOBL	fell outta bed laughing
FOD	fax on demand
FOIP	fax-over-Internet protocol
FOL	fact(s) of life
FOlnYaslf	fooling yourself
FOMCL	falling off my chair laughing
.FON	font; phone; phone directory (all file name extensions)
FOOBL	fell out of bed laughing
FOTCL	falling off the chair laughing
FP	fixed price
f.p.	freezing point
FPS	foot-pound-second
FR	family responsibility/ies
FRAG	fragment; fragmentation
FrEFone	free phone
Frm	from
FRS	farce
FrskyVxn	frisky vixen
FS	full scale
FS2S	from strength to strength
FSW	full-scale war
FT	flexi time
ft	foot
FTA	free-trade area
FTASB	faster than a speeding bullet
FTB	free-trade bloc

FTBOM<3	from the bottom of my heart
FTF	face-to-face
FTGF	fight the good fight
FT<30MB	from the heart of my bottom
FTK	first to know
FTL	faster than light
ft-lb	foot-pound
FTNIM	feel the need in me
FTT	free to talk (a statement of fact)
FTT?	are you free to talk? (a question)
FTZ	free-trade zone
FUD	fear, uncertainty and doubt
FUEO	for your eyes only
FURI	for your information
Fwd	forward
FWIW	for what it's worth
FX	special effects
FYaA	for your amusement
FYaI	for your information
FYEO	for your eyes only
FYI	for your information
FYIO	for your information only

G

G	grin
G2CU	glad to see you
G2G	got to go
G2GG	got to get going
G2SU	glad to see you
GA	go ahead
GAFIA	get away from it all
GAG	good as gold
gal	gallon
GAL	get a life
GAorStr8?	gay or straight?
GB	gigabyte; Great Britain; God bless!
GBH	grievous bodily harm
GBH&K	great big hug and kisses
GBH&KB	great big hug and kisses back
GBIP	general purpose interface bus
GBLF	Gays, Bisexuals, Lesbians and Friends (US)
gbln	goblin
GBU	the good, the bad and the ugly
GCHQ	Government Communications Headquarters
GCSE	General Certificate of Secondary Education
GD	gold digger
GD&R	grinning, ducking and running (after a snide remark)

GEkStnkBrth	geek stink breath
GEM	graphic environment manager
Gen	General
GENIE	General Electric Network for Information Exchange
GenX	Generation X
GEnysMov	genius move
GESP	generalized extrasensory perception
GetALIf	get a life
GetDwn2BiZniZ	get down to business
GetYaCotUvePuLd	
	get your coat you've pulled
GF	girlfriend
GG	good game
GGFN	gotta go for now
GGG	giggle
GGGG	good game, good game
GGN2DWI	God's got nothing to do with it
GHU	God help us
GHz	gigahertz
GI	good idea
GICSOS	glad I could help
GIGO	garbage in, garbage out
GiMETSunShIn	gimme the sunshine
GIU	get it up
GIWIST	gee, I wish I'd said that
GIX	Global Internet Exchange

GL	get lost; graphics language
GldALOva	glad all over
GLG	goofy little grin
GLoREDAz	glory days
GM	genetically modified
GMAL	give me a list
GMeMeYaLuvin	give me your loving
GMeSumLuvin	gimme some lovin'
GMex3	gimme gimme gimme
GML	generalized markup language
GMOs	genetically modified organisms
GMRT	give my respect(s) to
GMT	Greenwich mean time
GMTA	great minds think alike
Gn	grinning
Gna	gonna (going to)
GnaMkeUAnOFrUCntRfs	
	gonna make you an offer you can't refuse
GngGngGn!	going, going, gone!
GnIU	getting it up
GNO?	(did you) have a good night out?
GNVQ	General National Vocational Qualification
Go2	go to
Go4It	go for it
GOA	glad all over
GOAwALtleGrl	go away little girl
GOBak2YaPlnt	go back to your planet

67

GOd	good
GOdblBadTlms	goodbye bad times
GOdGOdGOd	good, good, good
GOdLuK	good luck
GOdLuvinAEz2Fnd	
	good loving ain't easy to find
GOdThngGoin	good thing going
GOdTlmsBeTaTlms	
	good times better times
GOdVibes	good vibrations
GOGOGOGOGOGOGO	
	go on, go on, go on, go on, go on, go on, go on
GOL	giggling out loud
Gonna	going to
GOOML	get out of my life
GOPlAlnTraFk	go play in traffic
GOT	gay old time
GotTTme?	got the time?
GotYaMojoWrkn	got your mojo working
GOWI	get on with it
GoYaOnWA	go your own way
GP	general practitioner
GQ	*Gentlemen's Quarterly* magazine
gr	grains; gross
Gr8	great; grate
Gr8B	Great Britain
Gr8r	greater; grater.

Gr8rGOd	greater good
Gr8st	greatest
Grmbo	grimbo
GrOp	group
GrO$	gross
GrOvy	groovy
GrOvyBaB	groovy baby
Grp	group
GrpEs	groupies
Grr	angry
GRUS	girls are us
GrwOldWivMe	grow old with me
GS	good service/sport
GSM	game, set and match
GSOH	good salary, own home; good sense of humour
GT	group technology; high-performance car (Italian, *gran turismo*)
Gta	gotta (got to)
GtaBASn	gotta be a sin
GTASW	goodbye, that's all she wrote
GTB	go to blazes
GTBOS	glad to be of service
GTBWDU?	go to blazes, why don't you?
GtBZ	get busy
GTCU	glad to see you
GTGFN	got to go for now

GtIt2gtha get it together

GtItOn get it on

GtItRIt get it right

GTMU good to meet you

GtOnUpGtOnDwn

get on up, get on down

GtOuTaMyDrms&In2MyLIf

get out of my dreams and into my life

GTREM going to read e-mail

GTRM going to read mail

GTRSM going to read snail mail

GTT go to town

GTTW go to the wall

GtUp get up

GUROHIO get your own house in order

GUTS grand unified theories

GV global village

GV4M good value for money

GVT global virtual time

GW gross weight

GWTOS go with the opposite sex

GWTSS go with the same sex

GYaHOMA get your hands on/off my assets

GYMOMT get your mitts off my tits

GYROHIO get your own house in order

H

H!	help!
H&K	hug and kiss
H&Kxx	hug and kisses
H&O	honestly and objectively
H&S	health and safety
H/W	Hardware
H2A	happy to accommodate
H2GN	have to go now
H8	hate
ha	hectare
HA!	hey!
HABABWan2GtLcky?	
	hey, baby, want to get lucky?
HACOIYOl	have a cool Yule
HAGN	have a good night
HAGOdLOkn	hey good looking
HAGT	have a good time
HAGT?	did you have a good time?
HAK	hugs and kisses
HAKxx	hug and kisses
HAL	heuristically programmed algorithmic (computer) (from 1968 movie *2001: A Space Odyssey*)
HaLeLuja	hallellujah

HAND	have a nice day
HaP	happy
HAP	hazardous air pollutant
HaP<3	happy heart
HaPDAz	happy days
HaPEANvrsrE	happy anniversary
HaPEBday	happy birthday
HaPEHolidAz	happy holidays
HaPEXmas	happy Christmas
HaPinS	happiness
HaPNdngGivYaslfAPnch	
	happy endings (give yourself a pinch)
HAQT	he's a cutie
HavAGOd4eva	have a good forever
HavAGr8DA8	have a great date
HavFnGoMad	have fun go mad
HavITRite?	have I the right?
HAZ	heat-affected zone
Hb	hemoglobin
HBH	hour by hour
Hbk	hardback
HC	health check
HCF	highest common factor
HCGE	he can't get enough
hcp	hexagonal close-packed
HCT	here comes trouble
Hd	had

HDEpIYRLuv?	how deep is your love?
HDIAU?	how does it affect you?
HDML	handheld device markup language
hdr	Header
HDTV	high-definition television
hdw	hardware
HDX	half duplex
HE	high explosive; His or Her Excellency; His Eminence
HedAbuvWata	head above water
HEP	hydroelectric power
HerCumsTSun	here comes the sun
HerCumTGOdTIms	
	here come the good times
HEX	hexadecimal
HF	high frequency
HFH	home from home
HGANBuT	he's got a nice butt
Hgh	high
HghNOn	high noon
HGNAbs	he's got nice abs
HGV	heavy goods vehicle
HH	double-hard (pencil lead); happy hour
HHH	triple-heard (pencil lead)
HHIS	hanging head in shame (not)
HHOJ	ha, ha, only joking
HIa&HIa	higher and higher

HIB?	have I been . . . ?
HIFD	high-density floppy disk
HIFllr	high flyer
HIH	His/Her Imperial Highness
HiHOps	high hopes
HIMEM	high memory
HIRT	hold it right there
HITAOME	he is the apple of my eye
HiThr	hi/hello, there
HITIms	high times
HITULThtILuvU?	have I told you lately that I love you?
HJ	hungry Joe
HJAM8	he's just a mate
.HLP	Help (file name extension)
HldMeClse	hold me close
Hle	whole/hole
HlpMeMkeItThruTNite	
	help me make it through the night
HlpYaSlf	help yourself
HLS	hook, line and sinker; hue, luminance, saturation (colour model)
HLuvWT	have love, will travel
HM	His/Her Majesty
HMG	His/Her Majesty's Government
HMI	His/Her Majesty's Inspectorate
HMM8	he's my mate
HMTDIH2TU	how many times do I have to tell you

HMTMKM hold me, thrill me, kiss me
HMTMKMxxx hold me, thrill me, kiss me lots
Hndbk handbook
HndK hug and kiss
HndKxx hug and kisses
HOD hunker on down
HOH hard of hearing
HOHILuv head over heels in love
HOldYaHEdUp hold your head up
HOLLAND hope our love lasts and never dies
HoLy holly
HoLywOd Hollywood
HON hour of need
HOpSt hope street
Hot4U hot for you
HotLuv hot love
HOTT *Hot Off The Tree* (electronic newsletter)
HotX3 (feeling) hot, hot, hot
HowWasIt4U? how was it for you?
HOYEW hanging on your every word
HP Hewlett-Packard; house party; hire purchase; have plenty
HPC handheld personal computer
HPCC high-performance computing and communications
HPDJ Hewlett-Packard Desk Jet
HPFS high-performance file system

HPG Hewlett-Packard Graphics
HPGL Hewlett-Packard Graphics Language
HPIB Hewlett-Packard Interface Bus
HPLJ Hewlett-Packard Laser Jet
HplSlyInLuvWivU
      hopelessly in love with you
HPnStnc happen stance
HPSIDOC HP Sauce is delicious, of course
HPUX Hewlett Packard Unix
HPyNYr happy new year
HPyXms happy Christmas
HR human resources
HRD human resource development
Hrdst hardest
HRG high-resolution graphics
HRH His/Her Royal Highness
HrHghnS Her Highness
HrsYaChnc2Gt2NoMe
      here's your chance to get to know me
HrTDrMMaGtWckd
      hear the drummer, get wicked
HS high speed; high street
HsHghnS His Highness
HSI hue, saturation, intensity
HSIK? how should I know?
HSP highly sensitive person; high-speed printer/processor

HTEI	hope this explains it
HTFP	hold the front page
HTH	hope this helps; hope to help
HTTP-NG	HTTP next generation
HTTPSR	HTTPServer
HU	Hacker's Utility (a famous hacking utility)
HUH?	have you heard?
HUR0	hold your own
H/V	horizontal/vertical
HVD	high voltage differential
Hvin	having
HvnIsAPlAcRItHerOnErth	
	heaven is a place right here on earth
HvnIsInYaHnds	heaven is in your hands
HVP	horizontal & vertical position
HwAbtU&IGtOutOfThseWetClthes?	
	how about you and I get out of these wet clothes? (after licking finger and touching yourself and her/him on shoulder)
HwDoULkMeSoFa?	
	how do you like me so far?
HWI4U?	how was it for you?
HYaS	have your say
Hz	has; hertz (cycles/sec)
HZ57	Heinz 57
Hznt	hasn't/has not

I

I&0	in and out
I4t	I thought
IAATR	I'm always at the ready
IABS	I am being sarcastic
IAC	in any case
IACpt	I accept
IACUC	if anyone can, you can
IAD	in all day
IAE	in any event
IAF	in a flash
IAFAQ	it's a fact
IAgrE	I agree
IAILA	I am in love again
IAILuv	I am in love
IAIMing	I am chatting with someone online
IAIMn	I am immediate; instant messaging
IAJOO	it's a jungle out there
IAK	I already know; I am knackered
IAL	internet address list
IALUVU	I'll always love you
IAM	in a moment/minute
IAMF	it's a minefield
IAMOS	in a manner of speaking

IAMSOProwdOfU
    I am so proud of you
IAN in all night
IANAL I an not a lawyer (but . . .)
IANALB I am not a lawyer but . . .
IANALBIPOOTN I am not a lawyer but I play one on the Net
IAON it's all over now
IAP Internet access provider
IARAW in a round about way
IAS in all seriousness; Internet access server
IATSITE it's all the same in the end
IAUP Internet user account provider
IAW in all week
IAWk in all week
IBElvInMrcls I believe in miracles
IBetUCntSwmUCldntKEpYaMthSht4LngEnuf
    I bet you can't swim, you couldn't keep your
    mouth shut for long enough
IBI I believe it
IBJ2T I'll be just two ticks
IBlveInMrclsUSxyThng
    I believe in miracles, you sexy thing
IBM idiots become managers; incredibly boring
    manual(s); International Business Machines
IBR it's been real
IBTC itty bitty titty committee
IBUD I bet you do!

ICAWS	I'm chanting as we speak
ICBW	I could be wrong
ICC2H	I couldn't care two hoots
ICCL	I couldn't care less
ICGE	I can't get enough
IC\GE	I can't get enough
ICI	I'm coming in
ICL	in Christian love
ICLW\U	I can't live without your love
ICLW\YRLuv	I can't live without your love
IC\MIT	I can't make it tonight
ICnLuvULkeTht	I can love you like that
ICntStndUBAB	I can't stand you baby
ICQ	I seek you (pron. phonetically)
ICRO	I'm coming right over
ICWenUXMe**	I see stars when you kiss me
ICTYBIWCYTF	I could tell you but I would claim you talked first; I could tell you but it would cause you to faint
ICTYBTIWHTKY	I could tell you but then I would have to kill you
ICU	I'll see you
ICUL8R	I'll see you later
ICUR	I see you are
ICW2CU	I can't wait to see you
ICW2CUL8R	I can't wait to see you later!
ICY	I'll see you

ICYL8R I'll see you later

IdDW\U I'd die without you

IdDW\YRLuv I'd die without your love

IDGI I don't get it

IDK I don't know

IDKWIG I don't know where I'm going

IdLOkGOdOnU I'd look good on you

IDM it doesn't matter

IDMM it's driving me mad

IDntACptTht I don't accept that

IDntAgrEWivTht

I don't agree with that

IDntGtIt I don't get it

IdntI2 I don't intend to

IdSa I'd say

IDTS I don't think so

I/F interface

IFA independent financial adviser

IfAPcturPntsKWrdsThnYCntIPntU?

if a picture paints a thousand words then
why can't I paint you?

IFD image file directory

IFDITD I feel down in the dumps

IFElLkePGyInTMDle

I feel like piggy in the middle

IfHeDsntShwUpImRtHre

if he doesn't show up I'm right here

81

IfIamWotRU? if I am, what are you?

IfISdUHdAButifulBdyWldUHldItAgnstMe?

if I said you had a beautiful body would you
hold it against me?

IFLD I feel let down

IfPoS if poss (possible)

IFU I feel you

IfUCntBWivT1ULuvLuvT1URWiv

if you can't be with the one you love, love
the one you're with

IfUGtaGoGoNowOrElseUGtaStaALNite

if you gotta go, go now or else you've gotta
stay all night

IfUHdABrAnuUdBDAnjrus

if you had a brain you would be dangerous

IfUWnt2AMndREdrTherWldBNoChrge

if you went to a mind reader there would be
no charge

IfYaMthWozNEBiGrUWdntHavNEFAcLft2Wsh

if your mouth was any bigger you wouldn't
have any face left to wash

IG2TLK it's good to talk

IGotUBbe I got you babe

Igr8i8 ingratiate

IGWTOS I go with the opposite sex

IGWTSS I go with the same sex

IH in hand

IH2BUWU	it had to be you, wonderful you
IH8U	I hate you
IHA	I hate acronyms
IHFU	I have fouled up
IHL	in human love
IHM	I hate mobiles
IHMP	I hate mobile phones
IHTFP	I have truly found paradise; I hate this flippin' place
IHTFU	I have truly fouled up
IHTM	I hate text messages
IHTP	I hate this place
IHTxtMsgs	I hate text messages
IHUHAGN	I hope you have a good night
II2	I intend to
IIAQ	I'm in a queue
IIARM?	is it a resigning matter?
IIN	it is now
IINHINW	if it's not hurting it's not working
IIRC	if I recall/remember/recollect correctly
IITYWYBAD?	if I tell you will you buy a drink?
IJC2SILuvU	I just called to say I love you
IK	I know
IKUHIIU	I knew you had it in you
IKUK	I know you know
IKWYABWAI?	I know what you are but what am I?
IKYABWAI?	I know you are but what am I?

ILA	image light amplifier
ILBAT	I'll be able to
ILBCnU	I'll be seeing you
ILBTher4U	I'll be there for you
ILCU	I'll call you
ILKEpYaDrmsAliv	I'll keep your dreams alive
ILkeYRCo	I like your company
ILLUIOTS	I'll let you in on the secret
ILLUIOTSIUPN2TA1E	
	I'll let you in on the secret, if you promise not to tell anyone else
ILTUWotIWanWotIRLyRLyWan	
	I'll tell you what I want, what I really, really want
ILU	I love you
I<3U	I love you
ILUVU	I love you
ILUVUMED	I love you more each day
ILuvUMorThnWrdsCnSa	
	I love you more than words can say
IM	immediate/instant message
ImBhndU100%	I'm behind you one hundred per cent
IMBLuv	it must be love
IMBO	in my biased opinion
IMCO	in my considered opinion
ImEV	I'm ever ready
ImEvrRdy	I'm ever ready

ImFrE!	I'm free!
Img	Image
ImGn	I'm grinning
Imgn	imagine
ImGoNaGtUSuka	I'm gonna get you sucker
IMH	in my hand
IMHO	in my humble opinion
IMi$MyTdyBerWldUSlEpWivMe?	
	I miss my teddy bear. Would you sleep with me?
IMi$nU	I'm missing you
IMi$U	I miss you
IMi$U2	I miss you, too
ImINEd0SLuv	I'm in need of some love
IMing	chatting with someone online usually while doing other things such as playing trivia or other interactive game
ImInIt4Luv	I'm in it for love
ImL0kn@U&IDntLIkWotIC	
	I'm looking at you and I don't like what I see
ImL0kn4AFrndDoUWan2BMyFrnd?	
	I'm looking for a friend. Do you want to be my friend?
IMn	immediate/instant messaging
IMNSCO	in my not so considered opinion
IMNSHO	in my not so humble opinion
IMO	in my opinion

IMOGT	in my own good time
IMOT	in my own time
ImpoS	impossible
ImRdy4Luv	I'm ready for love
IMS	I must say
Im*vin	I'm starving
ImA*vinRtst&Iwan2EatU	
	I'm a starving artist and I want to eat you
ImT14U	I'm the one for you
IMTV	interactive multimedia television
IMYaDstnE	I am your destiny
in	inch
In2	into/in to
INAOTTFLS	it's not all over till the fat lady sings
INEdU2Nite	I need you tonight
Info?	give me some information/details
ING2SIA	I'm not going to say it again
IN\GUTE	I'm not giving up that easily
INGUTE	I'm not giving up that easily
INI2	I never intended to
init	isn't it
INMBS	I need my beauty sleep
InMyABCIWldPutU&Itgthr	
	in my alphabet I would put you and I together
IN\N	it's not natural
INND	Internet News Daemon

INoUR	I know you are
INoUR1	I know you are one
INoWenURLIinYaLpsMov	
	I know when you are lying, your lips move
INPO	in no particular order
Inslts	insults
INTD	I'm not that desperate
INuUCldDoIt	I knew you could do it
IO	information overload
I/O	input/output
IOAT	I'm on a train
IOB2T	I'll only be two ticks
IOH4TB	I'm only here for the beer
IOHii4U	I only have eyes for you
IOL	information overload
IOOH	I'm out of here
IOP	input/output processor
IOTT	I'm on the train/tube
IOU	I owe you
IOU1	I owe you one
IOW	in other words
IOWAN2BWU	I only want to be with you
IPC	I'm past caring
IPN	I'm posting naked
IPng	Internet protocol, next generation
IPP	internet printing protocol
IQ	intelligence quotient

IQL	interactive query language
IQP2ABOT	I'm quite partial to a bit of that
IRC	Internet relay chat
IRC4U	I really care for you
IRL	in real life (when not chatting online)
IRQ	interrupt request
irradn	irradiation
IRSYHAFS	I remain, sir, your humble and faithful servant
ISAALTlPryr4U	I say a little prayer for you
ISC	I'm stir crazy; in some cases
ISdR	it's so de rigeur
ISI	in some incidences;
ISnIEr	I'm speaking in Engrish
ISO	in search of; inside-out
ISOTLuv	in search of true love
IS**WenUXMe	I see stars when you kiss me
IST	I said that
IsThtTBstUCanDo?	
	is that the best you can do?
ISUUHAvSchWLPwr	
	it's so unfair you have such willpower
IT	information technology
IT!	it's torture!
ITAFAQ?	is that a fact?
ItAntOvaTLItsOva	it ain't over 'til it's over
ITB	in the bank; in the beginning

ITCLOD	in the cold light of day
ITCOE	in the course of events
ITD	in the dark
ITE	in the end
ITEOTB	in the eye of the beholder
ITHOTM	in the heat of the moment
ITLOD	in the line of duty
ITMHO2U	I take my hat off to you
ItMstBLuv	it must be love
ITNOT	in the nick of time
ITP	in the pink
ITR	in the red; Internet Talk Radio
ITS	in the shade
ItsAMrcl	it's a miracle

ItsANuDAItsANuLIf

it's a new day, it's a new life

ItsEvry14ThmslvsThseDAs

it's everyone for themselves these days

ItsGOd2Txt	it's good to text
ItsNowOrNvr	it's now or never
ItsOnlEAGAmShO	it's only a game show
ItsSoEzE	it's so easy
ItsYaDstnE	it's your destiny
ItsYaLIf	it's your life
ItsYaTIm	it's your time
ITUFIR	I think you'll find I'm right
ITUM	I think you mean

ITYFIR	I think you'll find I'm right
IU2LUVUBIAON	I used to love you but it's all over now
IU2U	it's up to you
IU4I	I'm up for it
IUA	in your absence
IUC\STHTSOOTK	
	if you can't stand the heat then stay out of the kitchen
IUCWIM	if you see what I mean
IUDKIDKWD	if you don't know, I don't know who does
IUDO	I'm under doctor's orders
IUFI	I'm up for it
IUKW2DDI	if you know what to do, do it
IUKWIM	if you know what I mean
IUKWIMAITUD	if you know what I mean, and I think you do
IUR	it's under review
IURA	in your absence
IURG	if you're good
IURH	in your hand
IUSS	if you say so
IUSWIM	if you see what I mean
IUTLUVUBIAON	I used to love you but it's all over now
IvBinWtchnUNotWtchnMe	
	I've been watching you not watching me
IvSEnAHeltheaL0kinFAcOnAPIrtFlag	
	I've seen a healthier looking face on a pirate flag

IvSEnBeTaBoDsInACarBrkrsYrd
> I've seen better bodies in a car breakers yard

IvSEnMreHarOnA BlyudBL
> I've seen more hair on a billiard ball

IvSSILF I've started so I'll finish

IW Internet wars

IW2HYRBaBs I want to have your babies

IW4gtIt I will forget it

IW\4gtIt I won't forget it

IW\4gtYC I won't forget your kindness

IWADIWAN it wasn't a dream, it was a nightmare

IWan2WAkUpEvrEDAWivU
> I want to wake up every day with you

IWANU I want you

IWBAM I won't be a minute

IWBAS I won't be a second

IWBAT I won't be a tick

IWBJ2T I won't be two ticks

IWBNI it would be nice if

IWIK I wish I knew

IWiLSpk2UL8r I will speak to you later

IWIST I wish I'd said that

IWITOT I wish I'd thought of that

IWKUI I will keep you informed

IWL I was laughing

IWL&MM8WL I was laughing and my mate was laughing

IWLAlwysLuvU I will always love you

IWLD I was let down

IWldDiHPyIfISawUNkdJst1nc

I would die happy if I saw you naked just once

IWLIUWL I will if you will

IWLMM8WL I was laughing, me mate was laughing

IWLOL I was laughing out loud

IWntIUWnt I won't if you won't

IW\SaSo I wouldn't say so

IWTH I want to help

IWTHYRBaBs I want to have your babies

IYA in your absence

IYaF in your face

IYOGT in my own good time

IYRA in your absence

IYROT in your own time

J

J	joule
J2LUNILuvU	just to let you know I love you
J2T	just two ticks
JA	joking apart
JAM	just a minute
JAOTWR	just another off-the-wall remark
JAS	just a second
JAT	just a tick
JBOD	just a bunch of disks (like redundant array of independent disks, etc.)
JCO	just cuddle on
JCOT	just cuddle on tight(ly)
JFF	just with fun
JFK	John Fitzgerald Kennedy (35th President, USA)
JIC	just in case
JIT	just in time
JJ	just joking
JK	just kidding
JKOIT	just keep in on there
JLMA	just leave me alone
JM2p	just my two pennyworth
JOS	jolly old sort
JP	Justice of the Peace

JstADrmAwA	just a dream away
JstCLMe	just call me
JstP$nThru	just passing through
JstRmbaThtAnt	just remember that ant
JTJ	just the job
JTLUNoILuvU	just to let you know I love you
JTM	Je t'aime
JTT	just the ticket

K

K	thousand; kelvin
K8	Kate
KAIZEN	philosophy of constant improvement: KAI (Japanese for 'change'); ZEN (Japanese for 'good'):
KB	kilobyte
KBPS	kilobits per second
KBS	knowledge-based system
kb/S	kilobits per second
Ken	trendy plastic-looking boy (e.g Barbie's boyfriend)
KEpOnBlEvn	keep on believing
KEpOnBrnin	keep on burning
KEpOnPshn	keep on pushing
KEpTDrmAllv	keep the dream alive
kg	kilogram
KISS	keep it simple, stupid
KIT	keep in touch
KKK	Ku Klux Klan
KltZ	klutz
KMA$	kiss my ass
KMB	kiss my butt
KMI	keep me informed
KMRS	kiss my arse

KMT	Kuomintang
KndRgds	kind regards
KO	knock-out
KOIT	keep on in there
KOTC	kiss on the cheek
KOTL	kiss on the lips
kph	kilometres per hour
KS	kindred spirit
K$nW/Cnfdnc	kissing with confidence
KSRSR	que sera sera
KUTGW	keep up the good work
KUWTJ	keeping up with the Joneses
kV	kilovolt(s)
kW	kilowatt(s)
kWh	kilowatt hour(s)
KWIM?	know what I mean?
KX	a thousand kisses
KYaNOOI	keep your nose out of it
Kzn	*kaizen* (continuous improvement)

L	litre
L2BF	learn to be funny
L2K	last to know
L2R	left to right
L8	late
L8NiteOpn	late-night opening
L8r	later
L8rD	later, dude
lab	laboratory
LAB&TUD	life's a bitch and then you die
LAFOOW	like a fish out of water
LAL	loadsa love
LAm0	lamo
LAN	local area network
LardBckt	lard bucket
L@T	look at that
L@TO	late at the office
LAVM	leave a voicemail
LAX	Los Angeles International Airport
lb	pound (weight)
LBAC01T	let's be absolutely clear on one thing
LBBB	let bygones be bygones
LBC01T	let's be clear on one thing
LBJ	Lyndon Baines Johnson (37th President, USA)

LBN\L	last but not least
LBNL	last but not least
LBOGE	let's boogie
LBOGEOnDwn	let's boogie on down
LBW	leg before wicket
l.c.	in the passage etc. cited (Latin, *loco citato*); lowercase
LCAC	like chalk and cheese
LD	lethal dose
LDC	less developed country
LDR	long-distance relationship
LDRS	life doesn't run smoothly
LDYaW	let's discuss your wishes
LEnOnMe	lean on me
LEO	low Earth orbit
Les	lesbian
LEvIt	leave it
LEX	lexicon
LF	lady friend
LFA	Less Favoured Area
LGBT	lesbian, gay, bisexual and transgendered
Lge	large
LGS	loan guarantee scheme
LGW	low-graphics website
LHN	let's hope not
LI2M	leave it to me
LIB	let it be/begin

LIBK let it be known
LIBS let it be said/so
LIfLuvHaPinS life, love, happiness
LIFO last in, first out
LIfsACnch life's a cinch
LIk like
LIL last in line; let it last
listserv electronic mailing list used by discussion groups on the Internet
LItsOnDorOpnNo1In
lights on, door open, no one in
LItUpYaWrld light up your world
LivItUp live it up
LJBF let's just be friends
LkEU lucky you
LKIT like it
LLL lay, lady, lay; low-level language
LLOD last line of defence
LLTA lots and lots of thunderous applause
LMA leave me alone
LMAO laughing/laugh my arse/ass off
LMB leave me be
LMC lost my connection
LMD last man down; last-minute decision
LMI let me in
LMIOTS let me in on the secret
LMK let me know

LMKITM	let me know in the morning
LMMMC	let me make myself clear
LMMMU	let me make myself understood
Lmp	lump
LMS	let me speak
LNA	let's not argue
LNB	let's not bicker/bitch
LNGCA	let's not get carried away
LN\J2C	let's not jump to conclusions
LO	hello
LO!	look out!
LOALP	leaning on a lamppost
LOBL	lots of belly laughing
Loco	locomotive; train
LoILuvUWntUTLMeYaNme?	
	hello, I love you. Won't you tell me your name?
LOk	look
LOkWhsCmn	look who's coming
LOL	lots of luck; lots of laughs; laughing out loud
LOMBARD	loads of money but a right dickhead
LOnETUn	looneytune
L@@K	look
LOP	last orders, please
LOTJ	law of the jungle
LOTL	lie of the land
LOTP	leader of the pack

LOX liquid oxygen
LP long-playing record
LPR let's phone-race
LRF little rubber feet (the little pads on the bottom of displays and other equipment)
LS large scale
L&S large and small
LS! life sucks!
LSB lock, stock and barrel
LSD lysergic acid diethylamide
LSE London School of Economics
LSHNPN laughed so hard new pants needed
LSR least significant bit
LST let's save time
LTA lots of thunderous applause
LTC long time coming
LTEB let the entertainment begin
LTIC long time in coming
LtItB let it be
LTK last to know
LtLBtOfHvn little bit of heaven
Ltle little
LtLuvRul let love rule
LtLuvShIn let love shine
LTM laugh to myself
LtMeDrwUAPctur let me draw you a picture

LTNC	long time no see
LTR	long-term relationship
LtsB2gthr	let's be together
LtsCoOp	let's co-operate
LtsGet2gthr	let's get together
LtsGtHaPE	let's get happy
LtsHavABaL	let's have a ball
LTSI	let that sink in
LtsMkThsANite2Rmba	
	let's make this a night to remember
LtTFlAmBrnBrIta	
	let the flame burn brighter
LtTGOdTImsRoL	
	let the good times roll
LtYa<3Dns	let your heart dance
LtYaLuvFlO	let your love flow
LtYaslfGO	let yourself go
LU	London Underground
LUHN	let us hope not
LUL	love you lots
LULAB	love you like a brother
LULAS	love you like a sister
LUNA	let us not argue
LUNB	let us not bicker/bitch
LUNJ2C	let us not jump to conclusions
Luv	love
LUV2TLK	love to talk

LuvIsEvryThng love is everything
LuvIsTDrug love is the drug
LuvMeLuvMyDog
love me, love my dog
LuvMeWrm&Tndr
love me warm and tender
LuvMnsNvrHvin2SaYRSry
love means never having to say you're sorry
LuvOr0 love or nothing
LuvPEs&HrmnE
love peace and harmony
LuvsCum@U love's coming at you
LUVTLK love talk
LuvWLCnkrAL love will conquer all
LuvWLFndAWA love will find a way
LuvYa love you
LUWAM<3 love you with all my heart
LV luncheon voucher
Lw low
LW4gt lest we forget
LwDwn low down
LWH long way home
LWI loitering with intent
Lx love with a kiss
Lxx love and kisses

M

m	metre
M3Z	mobile-phone-free zone
M4I	mad for it
M8	mate
MaIEndThsSntncWivAPropstn?	
	may I end this sentence with a proposition?
MakItEzEOnYaslf	
	make it easy on yourself
MAkItHPn	make it happen
MAkItREl	make it real
MAkItSOn	make it soon
MAkMe!	make me!
MAkTWrldGoRnd	
	make the world go round
MAP	making a pass
MAPGGB	mine's a Pan-Galactic Gargle Blaster
math	mathematical(ly)
MAU	mad about you
Max	maximum
MBD	man bites dog
MBO	management by objectives
MBR	master boot record
MBURBMJ	My, but you're beautiful, Miss Jones
MBWA	management by walking around

MBX	mailbox
M&C	mediation and conciliation
MCC	Marylebone Cricket Club
MCP	male chauvinist pig
MD	most definitely
MDAL	mutton dressed as lamb
MDMA	methylene dioxymethamphetamine (ecstasy)
Me&U	me and you
Me4U	me for you
MEB	memory expansion board
Med	immediately
MES	makes excellent sense
metab	metabolism
mf	*mezzo forte* ('fairly loud')
MFI!	mad for it!
mfr	manufacturer; manufacture
MGB	may God bless
Mgr	manager; Monsignor; Monseigneur
MGt	maggot
M<3BlEds4U	my heart bleeds for you
M<3GO2U	my heart goes out to you
MHOTY	my hat's off to you
MI	mistaken identity
mi	mile
min	minimum; minute
MIPS	million instructions per second
MIS	make it so; maybe so; make it stop

Mi$	miss
Misc	miscellaneous
Mi$n	missing
Mi$nU	missing you
mixt	mixture
MkeMyDaSa+!	make my day, say yes
ml	millilitre(s); mile(s)
ML8r	more later; much later
MLLthed	mullethead
mm	millimetre(s)
MM8	my mate
MMD	make my day
MMDP	make my day, punk
MMI	man–machine interaction
MML8r	much more later; much, much later
MM0B	minding my own business
MNchkn	munchkin (short)
MndBdySol	mind body soul
MnDNmn	mind– numbing
MnEMAksTWrdGoARound	
	'Money makes the world go around'
MngBg	minge– bag (miser)
MNM	make no mistake
Mnsta	monster
Mnth	month
Mnthly	monthly
Mnths	months

Mny	money
mo	month
MOB	man overboard
Mob	mobile; mobile phone
MOB	mother of blonde
MoBDik	Moby Dick
MoD	Ministry of Defence
MODEM	modulator/demodulator
MOF	matter of fact
MOI	misuse of information
mol	molecule, molecular
MOM	major or minor
Mong	mongrel
MorF?	male or female?
MOSS	member of the same sex
MOTD	message of the day
MOTN	middle of the night; more often than not
MOTOS	member of the opposite sex
MOvnUpMOvnOn	
	moving up, moving on
MOvOUp	moving on up
MOvYaBdE	move your body
MowsbrAn	mousebrain
MP	Member of Parliament
mp	*mezzo piano* (fairly soft)
m.p.	melting point
mpc	megaparsec

MPDR	many people don't realize
mpg	miles per gallon
m.p.h.	miles per hour
MryMe	marry me
MRyXms	merry Christmas
MSB	most significant bit
MSBF	mean swaps before failure
Msg	message
MSG	monosodium glutamate
Msgs	messages
Mstrb8	masturbate
Mt	Mount
MTBCF	mean time between critical failures
MTBF	mean time before failure/between failures
MTE	my thoughts exactly
MTFBWU	may the Force be with you (sci-fi)
MTRM	make the right move
MTX	mobile telephone exchange
MU?	must you . . . ?
MUD	multi-user dimension
MUMBLE	multiple user multicast basic language exchange
MunE$$$£££MunE	
	money, money, money
MUSM	miss you so much
MUTEX	mutually exclusive
M&V	many and varied

MW	megawatt(s)
MWOSTU	my way of saying thank you
Mx	maxwell unit
MYaOB	mind your own business
MYaWK	make your wishes known
MYOB	mind your own business
MYROB	mind your own business
My2¢	my two cents (my opinion)

N

N not

N1! nice one!

N2CU2CUN nice to see you, to see you, nice

N2DBWU nice to do business with you

N2DWM nothing to do with me

N2G not too good

N2H nowhere to hide

N2K need to know (basis)

N2MU nice to meet you

N2N next to nothing

N2NiteJo not tonight, Josephine

N2R nowhere to run

N2T nowhere to turn

N2U next to you

n/a no account (banking); not applicable; not available

NAGI not a good idea

Nak not acknowledged (data transfer)

NANT not a nice thought

NATO North Atlantic Treaty Organization

NB note well (Latin, *nota bene*)

NB2D nothing better to do

NBD no big deal

NBD no big deal; night becomes day

NBM	nil by mouth
NBN	naughty but nice
NBTCBW	nothing's bad that can't be worse
NceDr$CnITlkUOutOfIt?	
	nice dress, can I talk you out of it?
nd	and
ND	New Deal
N&D	night and day
NDD	next door down
NDE	near-death experience
Ndl$Luv	endless love
Ndl$	endless
Ndl$Luv	endless love
NDN	next door neighbour
NDoin	not doing
NE	any
NE1	anyone
NE1WHdA<3WldNoThtILuvU	
	anyone who had a heart . . . would know that I love you
neg	negative(ly)
NEH	any how
NEM	any more
NEPlAc	any place
NET	any time; not enough time
Net	Internet
Nethng	anything

NEthngIsPSbl	anything is possible
NEthngUWan	anything you want
NETIm	anytime
NEW	any where
NEwer	any where
NEWn	any when
NEWS	north, east, west, south
N\F2T	not free to talk
NFD	next floor down
NFG	no flaming good
NFM	never works for me
NFU	next floor up
NFW	no feasible/flippin' way
NGA	no-go area
NGNJ	no gunk, no junk
N\gonna	not going
NGTCBB	nothing's good that can't be better
NGV4M	not good value for money
NH	nice hand
NHOH	never heard of him/her
NI@A	no idea at all
NIDW2C	no, I don't want to chat
NIFOC	naked in front of computer
NIFOCEM&Ms	naked in front of computer eating M&Ms
NIMBY	(someone who says) not in my back yard
NIMCO	not in my considered opinion
NIMHO	not in my humble opinion

NIMNSCO not in my not so considered opinion
NIMNSHO not in my not so humble opinion
NIMO not in my opinion
NiMWad nimwad
NL New Labour; not likely
NLB never look back
NLI not logged in
NM never mind
NME *New Musical Express* magazine
NMPKT not many people know that
NMPR not many people realize
NMS never more so
NN night-night
NNE north-northeast
NNW north-northwest
NO nice one
No number; know
NO1 no one
No1&0CnStopUNow
no one and nothing can stop you now
NOL national outlook
Nome gnome
NoMreMr/MsNG
no more Mr/Ms nice guy
NOn noon
NOWI not only will I . . .
NowIsTRItTIm now is the right time

NOYB	none of your business
NOYN	not on your nelly!
NP	no problem
N\P	no problem
NPC	not politically correct
NQA	no questions asked
Nrd	nurd
NRN	no reply/response necessary
NS	new style
NSN	never say no
NSNA	never say never again
NSPCC	National Society for the Prevention of Cruelty to Children.
NT2NITE	not tonight
NTIBOA	not that I'm bitter or anything
NTIM	not that it matters
NtlS	nevertheless
NTTT	never trust the Tories
NV4M	not value for money
Nva2L8	never too late
NvaEtMorThnUCanLift	
	never eat more than you can lift
NvaGivUp	never give up
NVC	nonverbal communication
NVQ	National Vocational Qualification
Nvr	never
Nvrmnd	never mind

NW	no worry/don't worry
NWNF	no win, no fee
Nxt	next
NxtDOr	next door
NYNY	New York, New York
NYP	not your problem

O

O	over (to you)
O!	oh!; over!
O!O!	Order! Order!
O2L	out to lunch
O2S	on to something
O2U	over to you
O4COL!	oh, for crying out loud!
O4GS!	oh, for goodness'/God's sake!
O4TC	out for the count
O&A	out and about
OAH	open all hours
OAO	on account of; old-age pension(er)
OASC	open-and-shut case
OBO	or best offer
obsd	observed
OBTW	oh, by the way
OBTWIAU	oh, by the way, I adore you
OD	open debate
ODA	online display of affection
OFM	often works for me
OFnsve	offensive
OFTC	out for the count
Ogr	ogre
OH	off hand; open house

OHMS	on Her/His Majesty's Service
OIC	oh, I see
OIL	options in law
OIN	oh, it's nothing
OJ	orange juice
OK	OK/okay
OL	old lady (girlfriend, wife, mother); online; outlook
OLA	online argument
OLAM	or leave a message
OLATT	online all the time
OLD	online divorce
OLL	online love
OLM	online marriage
OLR	online relationship/romance
OLRow	online row
OLS	online split
OLTS	Old Lady of Threadneedle Street (Bank of England)
OM	old man (boyfriend, husband, father)
On2	on to
ON4	on for
OnlETStrngSrvIv	
	only the strong survive
OnlyU	only you
OnlyU&Me	only you and me
ONNA	oh no, not again

o.n.o.	or near offer
ONUS	on an unrelated subject
OO	over and out
O&O	over and over; over and out
OO2U	options open to you
O&OA	over and over again
OOB	out of bounds
OOBE	out-of-body experience
OOH	out of hours
OOO	out of order
OOSOOM	out of sight, out of mind
OOT	out of touch
OOTT	out on the town/tiles
OOTW	out of this world
OOTWX	out-of-this-world experience
OPI	of paramount importance
OPnts!	oh, pants!
OpnUpYa<3	open up your heart
OpnUpYaMnd	open up your mind
OS	old style; on something
OT!	out there!
OTC	over-the-counter
OTF	off the floor
OTH	on the hour
OTOH	on the other hand
OTS	off the shelf
OTSOTM	on the spur of the moment

OTT	on the train/tube; over the top
OTTOMH	off the top of my head
OTTtt!	way over the top!
OTW	off the wall; on the whole
OU	Open University
OUAT	once upon a time . . .
OUATITW	once upon a time in the west
OutStndn!	outstanding!
outta	out of (here)
OW	offworld(er); oh well
OW2TE	or words to that effect
OWMG	oh well, mustn't grumble
OWntUStaJstALTIeBitLngr?	
	oh, won't you stay just a little bit longer
OWotAFElin	oh, what a feeling
OXFAM	Oxford Committee for Famine Relief
OYB!	on yer bike!
OYM	on your marks
OYMGSG!	on your marks, get set, go!
oz	ounce

P

P2G pretensions to grandeur
P3P Platform for Privacy Preferences Project
Pa pascal
PA personal assistant
p.a. per annum
PAB personal address book
PANS pretty awesome new stuff (as opposed to POTS)
PAW parents are watching
PAX private automatic exchange (telephony)
PAYE pay as you earn (taxation)
PBE prompt by example
PBJ peanut butter and jelly
Pbk paperback
PBRA please be/rest assured
PBX private branch exchange (telephony)
pc parsec
PC past caring; personal computer; phone card; Police Constable; politically correct
P&CA practical and constructive advice
PCB please call back
PCLI independent political entity (republic)
PCM please call me

PCMCIA people can't master computer industry acronyms

PctrThsUMeB%lesx2
picture this – you, me, bubble bath and champagne

pd paid

p.d. potential difference

PDA public display of affection

p.d.q. pretty damn quick

PDS please don't shoot

PE physical education

PEBCAK problem exists between chair and keyboard (it's the user's fault)

PeNEWls£FOlish
penny wise, pound foolish

PFC personal filing cabinet

PgDg pig dog

PGGB Pan-Galactic Gargle Blaster

PGP Pretty Good Privacy (encryption software)

PH Purple Heart

PHP personal homepage tool

PIBCAK problem is between chair and keyboard

PITA pain in the arse/ass

PITB pain in the bum/bottom/backside/butt

PITN pain in the neck

PITP pain in the posterior

PITR pain in the rear/rear end

PklP$	picklepuss
pl	place; plural
Pl8	plate
Pl2Win	play to win
PLC	public limited company
PLMKOK?	please let me know, OK?
Plnkr	plonker
PLS	please
PlsDntGo	please don't go
PM	postmortem; prime minister; private message
p.m.	post meridiem (afternoon)
PM4BR	pardon me for being rude
PM4BSRIWNMIWMFIJCU2SH&NIGBDB	
	pardon me for being rude, it was not me it was my food. It just came up to say hello, and now it's gone back down below.
PMFJIB	pardon me for jumping in but . . .
PMP	practice makes perfect
PMP	laughing my arse off and peeing my pants
PMP	peeing my pants
PmpItUp	pump it up
PmpUpTVolum	pump up the volume
PMWIBDMB	pardon me while I barf down my bra
POB	place of birth
Pobl	possible
POD!	party on, dude!
POETSDAY	push off early, tomorrow's Saturday

POM	peace of mind
POMM	piece of my mind
PONR	point of no return
::POOF::	goodbye (leaving the room)
POS	point of sale
PoS	possible
POT	plain old telephone
POTS	plain old telephone service
POV	point of view
POW	prisoner of war
powd.	powdered
pp	pages
pp	*per pro.* (by proxy)
pp	pianissimo (very softly)
p&p	post and packing
p.p.b.	parts per billion
ppl	people
p.p.m.	parts per million
PPP	Pariser-Parr-Pople; point-to-point protocol
PPS	Parliamentary Private Secretary; additional postscript
ppsig	pounds per square inch gage
ppt	precipitate
pptd	precipitated
pptg	precipitating
pptn	precipitation

PR	please reply; proportional representation; public relations
prep	prepare
prepd	prepared
prepg	preparing
prepn	preparation
PrfctDA	perfect day
PrfctWrld	perfect world
PRO	Public Record Office; public relations officer
prodn	production
PRs	mobile-phone races
PRS	pass (pron. as RP: 'pahs')
PRW	parents are watching
Prwn	prawn
PS	postscript; PlayStation
psi	pounds per square inch
psia	pounds per square inch absolute
PSX	PlayStation (Sony's entertainment system)
pt	pint
PTB	pass the bucket; please text back
Pte	Private
PTM	please text/tell me
PTO	please turn over
PTSB	pass the sick bucket
PTT	Pink Triangle Trust
PU!	that stinks!
PURMWURMI	put your money where your mouth is

PUTP	pick up the pieces
Pwr	power
Pwr2TPEps	power to the people
PwrTxt	power text
PYaTIM	put your trust in me
PYO	pick your own
PZaFAc	pizzaface

Q

Q	queue
QA	quality assurance
QBE	query by example
QBF	query by form
QBI	quite bloody impossible (RAF slang, said of flying conditions)
QC	quality circle; quality control; Queen's Counsel
QED	quite easily done; *quod erat demonstrandum* (which was to be demonstrated)
QEF	*quod erat faciendum* (which was to be done)
QF	quick-firing
QiTWIlURAhed	quit while you're ahead
QNQ	quantity not quality
QOL	quality of life
QOS	quality of service
QP	queer politics
qr	quarter(s)
QT	cutie
qt	quart(s)
q.t.	(on the) quiet
qual	qualitative(ly)
quant	quantitative(ly)
QuEr	queer

QuitWllURAhed
        quit while you are ahead

QUiTWllURAhed
        quit while you are ahead

      q.v. which see (Latin, *quod vide*)

  QWERTY standard keyboard (taken from top row of letters)

R

R	are
R2KUp	rushing to keep up
R4C	request for comments
RA	rest assured
1FM	Radio One (BBC)
RAG	red, amber, green
RAM	random-access memory
RAOK	random act of kindness
RARTMB	round and round the mulberry bush
RAT	relaxed attitude towards . . .
RB	ratbag
R&B	rhythm and blues; right button (of mouse)
RBBS	remote bulletin board system
RBC	red blood count
RBCS	Remote Bar Code System
Rch4TSky	reach for the sky
Rch4T****	reach for the stars
RckMeBaB	rock me, baby
R&D	research and development; rest and recreation
RDA	recommended daily allowance (dietetics)
RDAT	rotary-head digital audio tape
RdMyLps-ILUVU	
	read my lips – I love you

RECITE	Regions and Cities in Europe
redn	reduction
ref	reference
REM	rapid eye movements
reprodn	reproduction
RePTL	reptile
resoln	resolution
resp	respective(ly)
ResQMe	rescue me
ResQOTW	rescue is on the way
RFD1	right from day one
RFTS	reach for the sky; right from the start
RFT***	reach for the stars
RFTWG	right from the word go
RGBI	red green blue intensity
rgds	regards
RIP	*requiescat in pace* (rest in peace)
RIPs	rest in pieces
RIR	right is right
RIRWIW	right is right, wrong is wrong
RISTT	respectfully, I say to thee
RItHreRItNow	right here right now
RL	real life (that is, when not chatting)
RLC	right, left and centre
RLH	raving/right little Hitler
Rlx	relax
RM	read me; Royal Marines

RMB	ring my bell
Rmba	remember
RmbaURA*	remember you are a star
RmbaYaMne	remember you're mine
RMBR	remember
RML	read my lips
RMO	ring me on . . .
RMTxtMsg	read my text message (*as in* read my lips)
RNA	ring, no answer
ROCB	rolling on the carpet barfing
ROF	rolling on the floor
ROFL	rolling on the floor laughing
ROFLMAO	rolling on floor laughing my arse/ass off
ROFLUTS	rolling on the floor unable to speak
ROFLWTIMiis	rolling on the floor with tears in my eyes
ROFWivU	rolling on the floor with you
ROlTWrld	rule the world
ROP	right off planet
ROR	raffing out roud (Engrish for 'laughing out loud')
ROTBA	reality on the blink again
ROTF	rolling on the floor
ROTFL	rolling on the floor laughing
ROTFLABITC	rolling on the floor laughing and biting into the carpet
ROTFLHBO	rolling on the floor laughing his (her) butt off
ROTFLMAO	rolling on the floor laughing my arse off

ROTFLMAO&PMP
rolling on the floor laughing my arse off and peeing my pants

ROTFLMBO rolling on the floor laughing my butt off

ROTT right over the top

ROTTFL rolling on the floor laughing

ROYGBIV red, orange, yellow, green, blue, indigo, violet

RPG role-playing games

Rpulsve repulsive

R&R round and round

RRMTxtMsg reread my text message

RSI repetitive strain injury

RSM Regimental Sergeant Major

RSN real/really soon now

RSVP *répondez, s'il vous plaît* (please reply)

RSX real-time resource sharing executive

RTBF read the bloody FAQ

RTC round the clock

RTFM read the flipping manual

RTG radio-isotope thermoelectric generator

RTI read the instructions

Rtn return

RTS read the screen

RTS request to send

RTWU right there with you

RU are you?

RUF2T?	are you free to talk?
RUGAY?	are you gay?
RUOK?	are you OK?
RUOnMyWL?	are you on my wavelength?
RURdy2GoHmeNw?	
	are you ready to go home now?
RUReD2B<3Brkn?	
	are you ready to be heartbroken?
RUReD2Fll	are you ready to fly
RUT?	are you there?
RUTM	rather you than me
RUU4I?	are you up for it?
RUUP4IT?	are you up for it?
RUYaS	right up your street
RUYRS	right up your street
RWF	right way forward
RWHFY?	are we having fun yet?
RWTS	rough with the smooth
RX	receive/receiver
RXD	Received Data
RY	are you . . . ?
RYO	roll your own (write your own program; derived from cigarettes rolled yourself with tobacco and paper)
RYTM	rather you than me

S

s	second
S	shall not/shan't; should not/shouldn't
S1EE	someone else entirely
S1VS	someone very special
S2E	strive/ing to ensure
S2gthrAATY	still together after all these years
S2S	side to side; so to speak
S2SM	stand to suffer most
S2US	speak to you soon
S3Z	smoke-free zone
S4L	Spam for life (what you may get when you become someone's customer or client)
S8n	Satan
SA	Salvation Army; say; sex appeal; social airhead; start again; straight-acting
SA+!	say yes
SABENA	such a bad experience, never again
SAD	seasonal affective disorder
SaDO	saddo
Sadsak	sadsack
SAE/s.a.e.	stamped, addressed envelope
Salt&ILDoIt	say it and I'll do it
SAL	such a laugh
SAm2U	same to you

SAm2Uw/nobzon
same to you with knobs on

SAS Special Air Service; sticks and stones

SASWBMBBNCNHM
sticks and stones will break my bones but names cannot hurt me

SASWBMBBNWNHM
sticks and stones will break my bones but names will never hurt me

SATB start at the beginning

S@TB start at the beginning

S@T** staring at the stars

SBC single-board computer

SBF single black female

Sbk softback

SBT sad but true; screen-based telephone

SC\GE she can't get enough

SCAUAATY still crazy about you after all these years

SCGE she can't get enough

Schm0 schmo

ScmBg scumbag

SCNR sorry, could not resist

ScrE scary

SC$ success

SCS! success!

ScZBg scuzzbag

ScZBL scuzzball

SDC!	size does count!
SDM!	size does matter!
S&DS	specialized and dedicated service
SEG	smeg-eating grin
SEms	seems
Sen	Senator; senior
SEP	somebody else's problem
sepd	separated
sepg	separating
sepn	separation
SEsnsGrEtngs	season's greetings
SETE	smiling ear to ear
SETI	Search for Extraterrestrial Intelligence
sf	sforzando (with sudden emphasis – music)
SF	surfer-friendly (low-graphics website)
SFM	sometimes/seldom/somehow works for me
SF/sci-fi	science fiction
Sft	soft
SFX	sound effects; special effects
SFX	special effects; sound effects
SG	stop, go
SGS	still going strong
SH2SI	somebody had to say it
SHCOON	shoot hot coffee out of nose
shd	should
SHF	super-high frequency
SHID	slaps head in disgust

ShIn	shine
SHInLIkA*	shine like a star
ShInOn	shine on
ShLICaLUOrNdgU4Bfst2moro?	shall I call you or nudge you for breakfast tomorrow?
Shrta$	shortass
ShtUp	shut up
SINBAD	single income, no boyfriend, absolutely desperate (said mostly of females)
SIS	strength in specialization
SIT	stay in touch
SITAOME	she is the apple of my eye
SITD	still in the dark
SIYROB40	sleep in your own bed for once
SIz	size
SJAM8	she's just a mate
SK!	smoking kills!
Sk8	skate
Sk8r	skater
SkrwbL	screwball
Slav2Luv	slave to love
SM	snail mail
S&M	slave & master (sadomasochism)
SmIlURButiful	smile, you are beautiful
SmL	small
SmLeSox	smelly socks

SMM8 she's my mate

SM0 serious mode on

SMOFF serious mode off

Sm0kGtsInYaiis

    smoke gets in your eyes

SMS short messaging service

SN special needs

S&N stuff and nonsense

SNAFU situation normal, all fouled up

SNOBOL String Oriented Symbolic Language (programming language)

SO shut up; significant other; spot on

SOA start over again; state-of-the-art

SOB son of a bitch

SOD sad old drunk

SOE Special Operations Executive

SoFa so far

SOHF sense of humour failure

SoHwAmIDoin? so . . . how am I doing?

SoInLuvWivU so in love with you

SOIPE set out in plain English

SOL smiling out loud; strictly off limits

soln solution

SOM state of mind

SOME1 someone

SOMY? sick of me yet?

SOOL sorry, out of luck

Soons	as soon as
SoOutaLuv	so out of love
SOpa*	superstar
SOS	Save Our Souls (help!) – international distress signal
SOS8N	spawn of Satan
SOSImLstWchWA2YaPlce?	help, I'm lost. Which way to your place?
SOT	sort of thing
SOTA	state-of-the-art
SOTO	so often take over
SOX	sound exchange
SP	starting price; stop preaching
S&P	salt and pepper
SPA	sound, practical advice
SPK2ME	speak to me
SPQR	small profits and quick returns
SPTD	speak of the devil
sq	square
SRT	stay right there
SRy	sorry
SRySEms2BTHrdstWrd	sorry seems to be the hardest word
SS	Saints; seriously sad
S&S	sticks and stones
SS&BF	shipshape and Bristol fashion
SS><)))">	something smells fishy

SSIA	subject says it all
SSM	so sue me
Sstrs	sisters
St	Saint; street
ST	surf time
ST2MORO?	same time tomorrow?
STAATY	still together after all these years
StAnAllv	stayin' alive
StaWivMeBaB	stay with me, baby
STB	set-top box; spot the ball
STBY	standby/stand by
StckOnU	stuck on you
STD	sexually transmitted disease; spot the difference; subscriber trunk dialling
std	standard
StEd&MrsPEl	Steed and Mrs Peel
StEl	steel
STFW	search the flipping Web
Sth	something
SthLk	something like
StL	still
StLStndn	still standing
StndByYaMan	stand by your man
StndrdC	standard class
Stnkpot	stinkpot
StNNdMLLt	stunned mullet
STOL	short take-off and landing

StOl	stool
STR	short-term relationship
Str8DwnTLne	straight down the line
StrA	stray
StrngAsStEl	strong as steel
STrngEnuf	strong enough
StrtMOvn	start moving
ST:TNG	*Star Trek: The Next Generation*
STUD	shop until you drop
StUpd	stupid
STYD	shop until you drop
SU4M	stand up for me
Subj	subject
SUFID	screwing up face in disgust
SUIC	see you in court
Sum1	someone
SumTImSOn	some time soon
Sumwer	somewhere
SUN1IL2U	shut up, no one is listening to you
SurThng	sure thing
SVGA	super-video graphics adapter
SvnALMyLuv4U	saving all my love for you
SvnGrce	saving grace
SW	software; southwestern
SW?	so what?; says who?; since when?
SWAG	stupid wild-arse guess
SWAK	sealed with a kiss

SWALK	sealed/sent with a loving kiss
SWAX	sealed with a kiss
SWDTL	somewhere down the line
SWDURTW?	since when did you rule the world
SwEtDrEmsRMAdOfThs	
	sweet dreams are made of this
SwEtDrms	sweet dreams
SwEtInspr8shn	sweet inspiration
SwEtFrEdm!	sweet freedom!
SwEtSmLOfSC$	sweet smell of success
SWG	scientific wild guess
SWLXX	sealed/sent with loving kisses
Swmpbrth	swampbreath
SWNTL?	so what's not to like?
SWOT	strengths, weaknesses, opportunities, threats (business analysis tool)
SWR	short-wave radio
SWS	slow-wave sleep
SWXX	sealed with kisses
SWYaP?	so what's your problem
SWYP?	so what's your problem
SX	simplex signalling
SxA	sex appeal
SXS	step-by-step switching (telephony)
SXtrc	Scalextric

T

T2G	time to go
T2GGG	time to go, go, go
T2GX3	time to go, go, go
T2N	train to nowhere
T2SO	time to switch off
T3	trouble-free
T4A	together for always
T4AB	time for a break
T4ACB	time for a coffee break
T4ATB	time for a tea break
T4B	time for bed
T4LMK	thanks for letting me know
T4T	time for tea
T4TT	thanks for the thought
T8	(the) Tate
TA	Territorial Army
TA4N	that's all for now
TAF!	that's all, folks!
TAFN	that's all for now
TAH	take a hint
TAkIt2TLmt	take it to the limit
TAkItEzE	take it easy
TAkItHIr	take it higher
TAkYaTIm	take your time

TANLAD	there ain't nothing like a dame
TANSTAAFL	there ain't no such thing as a free lunch
TAO	take/taking account of
TARO	time's almost run out
TATW4NM	time and tide wait for no man
T/B	Top and Bottom
TBA	to be activated; to be advised; to be announced; to be arranged; to be assigned
TBBH	to be brutally honest
TBC	to be continued/confirmed
Tbg	tea bag
TB/GDGOd	the boy/girl done good
TBH	to be honest
TBIsYTCum	the best is yet to come
TBL	the bottom line
TBR	to be resolved
TBRS	the birds are singing
tbs	tablespoon
TBtchIsBak	the bitch is back
TBW	to be written
TC	take care; the sea; total commitment
T&C	terms and conditions
TCGE	they can't get enough
TCO	take control of
TD2U	totally devoted to you
TDcizunIsYas	the decision is yours
TDSS	time doesn't stand still

TDTU	totally devoted to you
TE	the end
TEAAT	the end and all that
Tee	T-shirt
Tele	television
TELEX	teletypewriter exchange
TeLItLIkItIs	tell it like it is
temp	temperature
TEXT	YELLING
TFA	together for always
TFAB	time for a break
TFACB	time for a coffee break
TFATB	time for a tea break
TFB	time for bed
TFC	the final countdown
TFH	thread from hell (online discussion that just won't die)
TFrdgHldsNoTRrs4U	
	the fridge holds no terrors for you
TFT	time for tea
TG	transgender
TGHAWFI	the Greeks have a word for it
TGIF	thank God it's Friday
TGInLuvWivY	this girl's/guy's in love with you
TGNI	the good news is
TGOdTBd&TUgly	
	the good, the bad and the ugly

TGr8C   take great care
ThAAntCEn0Yt   they aint seen nothing yet
thermodn   thermodynamic(s)
TherRPlntEMre><)))">ITC
        there are plenty more fish in the sea
TherRPlntEMrePBlsOnTBEch
        there are plenty more pebbles on the beach
Thmslvs   themselves
Thnk0fT££$$UVSAvd
        think of the money you've saved
ThnkThn   think thin
THNQ   thank you
ThrsAWrldOutSIdYaWnd0
        there's a world outside your window
ThruTPwr0fIntenshunUATrctALTWelthUNEOrDsir
        through the power of intention you attract all
        the wealth you need or desire
ths   this
Ths&Tht   this and that
ThsAM   this morning
ThsIsIt   this is it
ThsIsTDA   this is the day
ThsIsTRItTIm   this is the right time
ThsIsYaLif   this is your life
ThsLTlePGy   this little piggy . . .
ThsPM   this afternoon
tht   that

ThtDr$WldLOkGrtOnMyBdrOmFlr
	that dress would look great on my bedroom floor
ThtsAbFab	that's absolutely fabulous
ThtsFntstc!	that's fantastic
ThtSoKOl	that's so cool
THX	thanks
Ti2GO	time to go
TIA	thanks in advance (used if you post a question and are expecting a helpful reply)
TIADD2M	this is all double-Dutch to me
TIAII	tell it as it is
TIC	tongue in cheek
TIFM	take it from me
TiiHI	the ayes (I's) have it
TIm4Acshun	time for action
TIME	tears in my eyes
TINWIS	that is not what I said
TIOLI	take it or leave it
TIY	that is why . . .
TJS	the January sales
TK	telekinesis

TkeAChnceOnMe?

take a chance on me?

TkeMyHndTkeMyHleLfe2CosICntSOSFLnInLuvWivU

take my hand, take my whole life, too, 'cos I can't help falling in love with you

TL till/until

TLA three-letter acronym

TLC tender loving care

TLItsROnBtNo1IsHOm
the lights are on but no one is home

TLK talk

TLK2ME talk to me

TLK2UL8R talk to you later

TLK2YAL8R talk to you later

TLK2YL8R talk to you later

TLKn talking

TLMeImDrmn tell me I'm dreaming

TLMIMW the law/Lord moves in mysterious ways

TLNE the list never ends

TlstTImISawLegsLIkThtTherWozAMSgTId21OfThm
the last time I saw legs like that there was a
message tied to one of them

T&M time and motion

TM2F tailor made to fit

TMB text me back

TMC too many cooks

TMCSTB too many chefs spoil the broth

TMI too much information

TMINET too much information, not enough time

TMIY take me, I'm yours

TMO text me on . . .

TMOL the meaning of life

TMS	tailor-made solution
TMWBTC	that may well be the case
TNN2S	there's no need to shout
TNO	the nature of
TNOTVS	there's nothing on TV, so . . .
TO	time out; too
TOL	tub of lard
TOML	time of my life
TOnlEWAIsUp	the only way is up
TOnlyThngThtLOksGOdOnMeIsU	
	the only thing that looks good on me is you
TOPCA	till our paths cross again (early Celtic chat term)
TOrg	toerag
TOTBE	that's only to be expected
TOTP	*Top of the Pops*
TOTP2	*Top of the Pops 2*
TOTT	totally over the top
TOU	thinking of you
TOY	thinking of you
TPONR	the point of no return
TPRE	the possibilities are endless
TpsyTrvy	topsy-turvy
TPTB	the powers that be
TPTP	the phrase that pays
TPwrIsYas	the power is yours
TQM	total quality management

TR14U	the right one for you
TRH	Their Royal Highnesses
TRiteTOl4Tjob	the right tool for the job
TrLL	troll
Trndoid	trendoid (trendy but robotic)
TRNN	the Richard Nixon rule
TrnUpTPwr	turn up the power
TRO	time's run/running out
TruLuv	true love
TS	time scale; transsexual; typescript
TSFF	that's so far-fetched
TSIzURIBetUHavYaOwnPstCOd	
	the size you are, I bet you have your own post code
TSNE	the story never ends
TSooooU!	that's soooo unfair!
Tsp	teaspoon
TSS	typescripts
TT	the Tube; think tank; teetotal; teetotaller
T&T	trials and tribulations; tried and tested
TT4N	ta-ta for now
TTBE	that's to be expected
TTD	today's the day
TTEOAN	through the eye of a needle
TTFN	ta-ta for now
TTG	time to go
TTGGG	time to go, go, go

TTIAO	they think it's all over
TTImHsCum	the time has come
TTL	through the lens
ttl	total
TTL4N	that's the lot for now
ttlty	totality
ttly	totally
TTn	think-tanking
TTOML	the time of my life
TTOYaL	the time of your life
TTT	thought that, too (when someone types in what you were about to type)
TTTD	ten to the dozen
TTTS	too tired to snog
TTUL	talk to you later
T&TW4NM	time and tide wait for no man
TTYL8r	talk to you later
TU	thank you
TU4YaH	thank you for your help
TULE	took you long enough
TUVLURWEL	thank you very little, you're welcome even less
TUVM	thank you very much
TV	television; transvestite
TVBOL	the very best of luck
TWDN	that will do nicely
TWE	time without end

TWhElsMvnBtTHmstrsDEd	the wheel's moving but the hamster's dead
TWIMC	to whom it may concern
TWIS	that's what I said
TWMA	till we meet again
TWTT	the worm that turned
TWUA*	to wish upon a star
TWUT	that's what you think
Txt	text
Txt3Z	text-free zone
TxtLnd	Text Land
TxtMeBaB	text me, baby
TxtMsgRg	text-message rage
TxtOvrld	text overload
TxtSpEk	text speak
TYaL4N	that's your lot for now
TYVM	thank you very much
TZ	*The Twilight Zone*

U

U	you
U2D	up to date
U2MeREvryThng	
	you to me are everything
U2TM	up to the minute
U2TS	up to the second
U2U	up to you
U4IT	up for it
U4Me	you for me
UAD	you always do
UAN	up all night
U+Me=Luv	you plus me equals love
UAPITA	you're a pain in the arse
U@?	where are you?; where are you at?
UBlwMyMnd	you blow my mind
UBM<3	you break my heart
UBMH	you break my heart
UBrnFatEFrtlSlE	
	you burn fat effortlessly
UBS	you'll be sorry
UCAROM	you can always rely on me
UCBS	you can't be serious
UCCL	you couldn't care less
UCDI!	you can do it

UCGE you can't get enough

UCldGetAJobAsADcoy4AWAlinShp

you could get a job as a decoy for a whaling ship

UCldSwatFlIsW/thseErs

you could swat flies with those ears

UCLIU you can look it up

UCLOM you can lean on me

UCMI you can make it

UcnDoItIfUOnlEThnkUCan

you can do it if you only think you can

UCnDoMgic you can do magic

UCnGtItIfURELEWan

you can get it if you really want

UCnHavItAL you can have it all

UCnNevaB2RichOr2Thn

you can never be too rich or too thin

UCSFTT you can't say fairer than that

U&D up and down

UDntHav2SaULuvMe

you don't have to say you love me

UDntNoTMninOfTWrdFearInFctUDntNoTMninOfALotOfWrds

you don't know the meaning of the word fear; in fact you don't know the meaning of a lot of words

UDO under doctor's orders

UDontNEdOInsted

you don't need anything to replace cigarettes

UDoSumthng2Me

you do something to me

UDsrveSCe$ you deserve success

UFascin8Me you fascinate me

UFLT you frisky little thing

UFM usually works for me

UFO unidentified flying object

UFVU you frisky vixen, you

UGetWUxpctNtWUDsrvXpctTBEST

you get what you expect, not what you
deserve – expect the best

UglE ugly

UGoTaBlEv you gotta believe

UGotIt you got it

UGotSOl you got soul

UGotTPwr you've got the power

UGtTPwr you've got the power

UGtWotItTAks you've got what it takes

UH2BT you had to be there

UHavARIt2BfrE

you have a right to be free

UHavARIt2Bluvd

you have a right to be loved

UHavFAthInYaSlf

you have faith in yourself

UHBW	you have been warned
UHL	you have lost
UKWIM	you know what I mean
UKWUCD	you know what you can do
UL@@KDITD	you look down in the dumps
ULD	you'll do
ULDITD	you look down in the dumps
ULiteMyFre	you light my fire
ULOkGr8&FElGr8	
	you look great and feel great
ULOkLIk$1MALGrEn&RinklE	
	you look like a million dollars – all green and wrinkly
ULOkTRFicInASwmsuit	
	you look terrific in a swimsuit
U&Me	you and me
UMHXRayii	you must have X-ray eyes
UMI	you made it
UMMV	your mileage may vary (you may not have the same luck I did)
UND	you never do/did
UNM	under new management
UNNF	you need never feel . . .
UNoWotUCnDo	you know what you can do
UOH2A	you only have to ask
UP	Unwired Planet
Up2	up to

Up2Scrtch up to scratch

Up2U up to you

UR under review; you are; your

UR1SndwchShrtOfAPiKnk

you are one sandwich short of a picnic

URA you are affectionate

URAFctionte you are affectionate

URAFInanshal-=#:-)

you are a financial wizard

URAGD you are a gold digger

URALEnMEnMchEn

you are a lean mean machine

URAL<3 you are all heart

URAnACdntWAtn2HPn

you are an accident waiting to happen

URAnInspir8shun

you are an inspiration

URAsMchUsAsMdGrdsOnATortus

you are as much use as mudguards on a
tortoise

URA*NactLIk1 you are a star, now act like one

URAsUsfLAsAChocl8Tpot

you are as useful as a chocolate teapot

URATA you are a tight arse

URBtifl you are beautiful

URCalm&:-)) you are calm and cheerful

URDMM you're driving me mad

URFleSBrAv&Bold
　　　　you are fearless, brave and bold
URGr8 you are great
URGr8nOnMyNrvs
　　　　you are grating on my nerves
URGrgus you are gorgeous
URGTnBeTa&BeTa
　　　　every day in every way, you are getting
　　　　better and better
URL universal (or uniform) resource locator
URL8D you're late, dude
URLI you're losing it
URLIkTVnusDMlloVBtiflBtNotALTher
　　　　you are like the Venus de Milo – very
　　　　beautiful but not all there
URLoco! you are crazy/mad
URLuv you are love
URMNO1 you're my number one
URN you are not
URNE2UT you are not expected to understand this?
URNtAlOn you are not alone
UROl! you rule!
UROnMyWL you are on my wavelength
UROYaO you're on your own
URR urgent reply required
URS you arse
URS4EVR yours sincerely for ever

URSchA*   you are such a star
URSF   yours faithfully
URSoMEnTQunBlnksWenUOpnYaWaLT
        you are so mean the Queen blinks when you open your wallet
URSOOldUCnRmbaWenMdmeBuTrFlyWasOnlyACatrpLa
        you are so old you can remember when Madame Butterfly was only a caterpillar
URSOOldUCnRmbaWenMoBDikWozOnlyATdPOl
        you are so old you can remember when Moby Dick was only a tadpole
URSOOldUCnRmbaWenTDedCWasJstIL
        you are so old you can remember when the Dead Sea was only ill
URSOShrtIfUPuLdUpYrSoxUdBBlndfld
        you are so short that if you pulled up your socks you would be blindfold
URSS   yours sincerely
URT   you are tight
URT1   you are the one
URT4CBhndTPwr
        you are the force behind the power
URTAOME   you are the apple of my eye
URTBstThngThtsEvrHPnd2Me
        you're the best thing that's ever happened to me
URTGr8st   you are the greatest

URTTops	you are the tops
URUDO	you're under doctor's orders
URVW	you're very welcome
URVWIA	you're very welcome in advance
URW	you're welcome
URWIA	you're welcome in advance
URWlcm	you're welcome
URWrm&Luvabl	you are warm and lovable
URX:-"	you are an ex heavy smoker
URX:-Q	you are an ex smoker
USB	universal serial bus
USD	upside down
USENET	users' network – bulletin boards on the Internet
UTC	under the circumstances
UTLKIN2ME?	you talking to me?
UTMeREvrythng	you to me are everything
UUDO	you're under doctor's orders
UV	you've
Uve	you've
UVG2BK	you've got to be kidding
UvGotAFAcLIkASqEzdTBag	
	you've got a face like a squeezed tea bag
UvGotANIcPrOfLgsSpeciallyTLft1	
	you have got a nice pair of legs especially the left one

UvGotMreChnsThnAChInEsFOnBOk

you've got more chins than a Chinese phone book

UW you're welcome

UWnAgn you win again

UWST you'll show them

UWUWUWUWUWUWUW

you will, you will, you will, you will, you will, you will, you will

UWWI you will walk it

UXB unexploded bomb

V

V	volt
V4M	value for money
VAT	value-added tax
VBG	very big grin
VBSEG	very big smeg-eating grin
VeGe	veggie (vegetarian)
VH	virtual hug
VIP	very important person
VK	virtual kiss
VM	voicemail
vol	volume
VPM	very private message
VR	virtual reality
vs/v	versus
vv	verses; volumes
VVCAMCS?	voulez-vous couchez avec moi ce soir?
Vxn	vixen

W

W	watt
W/	with
W	will not/won't; without; would not/wouldn't
W1WF	witless one-word follow-up
W2B4	what to budget for
W3C	World Wide Web Consortium
W4M	wait for me; works for me
W4MT	wait for me there
W8	wait
W84Me@	wait for me at . . .
W8n	waiting
WA2	well able to . . .
Wadya	what do you . . . ?
WAEF	when all else fails
Wak0	whacko
WALOOR	what a load of old rubbish
WAN2	want to
WAN2TLK?	want to talk?
WANA	we are not amused
WAQuErDo	what a queer do
WASP	White Anglo-Saxon Protestant
WAWTG!	what a way to go!
WB	welcome back

WBO	with bells on
WCB	will call back
wd	would
WDALYIC?	who died and left you in charge?
WDHTHLL?	what does he think he looks like?
WDSTSLL?	what does she think she looks like?
WDTTTLL?	what do they think they look like?
WDU?	why don't you . . . ?
WD\U?	why don't you . . . ?
WDUMBT?	what do/did you mean by that?
WDWWH2	we did what we had to
WDYAP	well do ya, punk?
We@	we are at . . .
WEBCAM	Web camera
WebP	Web phone
w.e.f.	with effect from
WenCnICUAgn?	when can I see you again?
WenEvrULOkUpTherShLIB	
	whenever you look up there shall I be
WenILOkIntoYaiisIenCNo1isDrIvin	
	when I look into your eye I can see no one is driving
WeR@	we are at . . .
WerRU?	where are you?
Werv u bin?	where have you been?
WF	wallflower; Web favourite
WFM	works for me

W\G	without guilt
WGRT	with greatest respect(s) to
WGT?	who goes there
WHAGOT	we/we've had a gay old time
whr	where
WhrRU@?	where are you at?
whrRUNow?	where are you now?
WhrTNow?	where are they now?
WIAN?	what's in a name?
WIBNI	wouldn't it be nice if
WICIWIW	what I see is what I want
WILG2TFOOAS	well, I'll go to the foot of our Auntie's stairs
WIR	when in Rome
WISIWIW	what I see is what I want
WISRR!	when I say run . . . run!
WIST	wish I'd said that
WIT?	what is that?
WITM?	what is the matter?
WITOT	wish I'd thought of that
WITT	we're in this together
Wiv	with
Wiv	without
Wivin	within
Wivout	without
WIW	wrong is wrong
Wk	week
Wkly	weekly

Wknd	weekend
Wkndr	weekender
Wkndrs	weekenders
Wknds	weekends
WL	wavelength
Wlcm	welcome
WLDne!	well done

WldULkeSum12GoWivYaDrnk?
would you like someone to go with your drink?

WldULkeTPlsreOfMyCo?
would you like the pleasure of my company?

WLGoTaDw/I	what's luck got to do with it
WlkOnAr	walk on air
WlkOnSnShIn	walk on sunshine
WLSpk2UL8r	will speak to you later
WLUBAB	who loves you baby
WLUMRyMe?	will you marry me?
WLUMRyMe?	will you marry me?

WLUStLLuvMe2moro?
will you still love me tomorrow?

WLWTCDI	well, look who the cat dragged in
WMGRT	with my greatest respect(s) to
Wmp	wimp
WMRT	with my respect(s) to
W/o	without
WOA	work of art

WOG	without guilt
WOLOGOMBA	without loss of generality, one may be assured (that...)
WOM	word of mouth
WORM	write once, read many
WOT	waste of time
Wot?	what?
WotCnIDo2MkeUMne?	
	what can I do to make you mine?
WOTT	way over the top
Woublt	would you be able to . . . ?
WP	whoever/whenever/wherever/whatever/ whichever possible; word processor/ processing
w.p.m.	words per minute
WR2	with respect to
wrd	word
WrdprcSr	word processor
Wrk	work
WrkBOK	work book
Wrkout	workout
WrkOvr	work over
WrkThtMagc	work that magic
WRS	work-related stress
WRT	with respect(s) to
WRUL0kn@4ii?	
	what are you looking at four-eyes?

WS	web store
WS	website
Wshn&Hpn&Thnkn&Prayn	
	wishing and hoping and thinking and praying
WSLS	win some, lose some
WSP	wireless session protocol
WSTD!	well, shut that door!
wt	weight
WT?	what/who the?
WT?	what's that?
Wt4MeDrln	wait for me, darling
WTB	wanted to buy
WTG!	way to go!
WTGP?	want to go private?
WTH	want to help?; what/who the heck; what the hell
WTM?	what's the matter?
WTOS	with the opposite sex
WTSS	with the same sex
WTTW	word to the wise
WU?	what's up?
WUBS?	will you be sad?
WUBT?	will you be told?
WUCBWH	wish you could be here
WUCIO?	will you cut it out?
WUCIWUG	what you see is what you get
WUET?	will you phone home?

WUF?	where are you from?
WUJL?	will you just listen?
WUJSUAL?	will you just shut up and listen?
WUMM?	will you marry me?
WUPH?	will you phone home?
W\USaSo	wouldn't you say so?
WUWH	wish you were here
WVA	well-versed argument
WW	worldly wise
WW1/WWI	World War One
WW2/WWII	World War Two
WWM	*Watch With Mother*
WWOTT	way, way over the top
WWW	World Wide Web
WWW	World Wide Web; Why? Why? Why?
WWWHT	well, who would have thought
WWWOTT	way, way, way over the top
WYaP?	what's your point?
WYaSOH?	where's your sense of humour?
WYSBYGI	what you see before you get it
WYSIWYG	what you see is what you get

X

X	kiss
xclusv	exclusive
xclusvly	exclusively
XclusvlyYRS	exclusively yours
XCOPY	extended copy
XcusMe?	excuse me?
XcusMeCnUGivMeDrctns2Ya<3?	
	excuse me, can you give me directions to your heart?
XF	X File
XFER	Transfer
XL	extra large
XLAT	translate
XInt	excellent
XLnt	excellent
XMA	kiss my arse
XMe	kiss me
XMeQk	kiss me quick
XMeSlwly	kiss me slowly
XMIT	transmit
XMRS	kiss my arse
XMTR	transmitter
XO	executive officer
XOFF	transmitter off

XON	transmitter on
XOTC	kiss on the cheek
XOTL	kiss on the lips
Xoxoxoxo	hugs and kisses
XPORT	transport
XREF	cross-reference
Xtreme	extreme
Xtrmnte	exterminate
Xxx	kisses
XYZ	examine your zip/zipper
XYZPDQ	examine your zipper pretty darn quick

Y

Y2MeREvrythng
> you to me are everything

YA yet another

Ya your

YABA yet another bloody acronym

YaBestISGOdEnuf
> your best IS good enough

YaBrthIsSwEt&YaLngsRClr
> your breath is sweet and your lungs are clear

YaBumLOksBigInTht
> your bum looks big in that

YaConfdnceShwsOnYaFAc
> your confidence shows on your face

YaFEtRSoBigUCldStmpOutBushFIrs
> your feet are so big you could stamp out
> forest fires

YaFOC you're full of clichés

YaiisRLIkPOls – MuDyPOls
> your eyes are like pools – muddy pools

YaLiftDsntREchTTopFlOr
> your lift doesn't reach the top floor

YaMemresSoBadYaMamaUsed2rapYaLnchInARdMap
> your memory's so bad your mother used to
> wrap your lunch in a road map

YAPITA you're a pain in the arse

YaShpIsCuMnIn
        your ship is coming in

Yaslf yourself

YaTEthRLIkT**sThyCumOut@Nite
        your teeth are like the stars, they come out at night

YaTImHsCum your time has come

YB yearbook

YBMH you break my heart

YBS you'll be sorry

YCCL you couldn't care less

YCGE you can't get enough

YC\GE you can't get enough

yd yard

YdLOd wide load

YD\U? why don't you . . . ?

YFLT you frisky little thing

YFVY you frisky vixen, you

YG young gentleman

YHM you have mail

YKWYCD you know what you can do

YL young lady

YL@@KDITD you look down in the dumps

YLD you'll do

YLDITD you look down in the dumps

YM young man

YMMV	your mileage may vary (you may not have the same luck I did)
YMN01	you're my number one
YN?	why not?; why now?
YngFrE&Sngl	young free and single
YOB	year of birth
YOYO	you're on your own
YPEPuP	yuppie puppy (new rich kid)
yr	year; your
YRDMM	you're driving me mad
YRGR8	you are great
YRL8D	you're late, dude
yrly	yearly
YRM	your move
YROnMyWL	you are on my wavelength
yrs	years
YRS	you arse
YRS4EVR	yours for ever
YRSF	yours faithfully
YRSS	yours sincerely
YRT	you are tight
YRTAOME	you are the apple of my eye
YRUDO	you're under doctors orders
YTLKINTME?	you talking to me?
YUDO	you're under doctor's orders
YUPPIE	Young Urban (or Upwardly mobile) Professional (person)

YVW	you're very welcome
YVWIA	you're very welcome in advance
YW	you're welcome; young woman
YWIA	you're welcome in advance
YYSSW	yeah, yeah, sure, sure, whatever

Z

Zng!WntTStrngsOfMy<3
               zing! went the strings of my heart
       Zt zit (spot)
   ZTFAc zitface
   Zzzz I'm bored/boring; I'm tired

EMOTICONS

-!-!-!	NO! NO! NO!
'!	grim
-!	no
-!!	definitely not
!-(	I'd like to thank whoever gave you that black eye
!¬(	a black eye
"	sour puss
-"	whistling casually
#:-)	smiling with a fur hat
#:-0	oh, no!
$	double S
%	double B
%-)	cross-eyed; I am drunk but happy
%*@:-(	I am hung over with a headache
%-}	intoxicated
%+{	you are a loser
%-<I>	I am drunk with laughter (not)
%-6	not very clever
&:-)	smiling with curls
&:-]	you are very handsome with square jaw
(: -)	URClvr! good luck in your exams
(:+(	ooh I'm scared
((_0_))	fat arse

((H)))	a big hug
(-)	get your hair cut
(\'.\')	a dog
(-.-)ZZzz	a dog asleep
(-:	also smiling; smiling back; I am left-handed
(:-&	angry
(:-)	shame you lost the last hair; smiling with helmet
(:-{~	the beard really suits you
(:-|K-	this is a formal message
(:-...	I am heart-broken
(:-D	blabber mouth
(@ @)	you're kidding!
(]:-)	I am gung ho
(^o^)	I am joyously singing your praises
(-_-)	this is my secret smile (sideways)
(_,,_)	fat arse
(_?_)	dumb arse
(_o_)	an arse that's been around
(_0_)	an arse that's been around even more
(_x_)	kiss my arse
(><)	you are anally retentive
(c:	bloke/bunny with big nose
(C:	smiling big nosed bloke
('o')=***	a dog barking
(0—<	fishface
)|-[	you are tired, grumpy and very sad

)i({	butterfly
*	star
**	stars
**-(	I am very, very shocked
:/I	well done you've stopped smoking!
**ITE	stars in their eyes
*:-o	someone who is really scared
*:0)	bozo
*^_^*	a huge dazzling grin
*<8-)X	why don't you wear your fantastic new party outfit with hat and bow tie
B	blink
G	giggle or grin
H	hug
L	I am blotto (sideways)
S	sob
W	wink
X	kiss
.^,	I am looking sideways/happy
.o+I)=:	a ballerina
.o+I)=::	a ballerina standing on tip toes
-/-	you are a stirrer
/0\	I am ducking
:-(	sad
:-)	happy
:-))	cheerful
:-)))Xmas	happy Christmas

: (:)	you pig!
:')	happy and crying

:-) &L0kEmInT iis

        smile and look 'em in the eyes

:-)))	very happy
:-)))ANvrsrE	happy anniversary
:-)))BrthdA	happy birthday
:@	shouting
:t	pouting
:!	foot in mouth
:-"	heavy smoker
:-#	my lips are still sealed
:#)	I am drunk every night
:-#|	I love the bushy moustache
:-$	put your money where your mouth is
:-%	merchant banker
:-&	I feel tongue-tied
:-(	boo hoo
:'-(	crying; I am crying
:-(	sad
:(	sad, without nose
:-()	shocked; smiling with mouth open

:-(YaBrAnIsntAsBgAsYa (_,,_)

        what a pity your brain isn't as big as your bottom

:-0	give me a snog
:-(*)	that comment made me sick

:(*)	you make me sick
:-(~~	I'm sick; I've been sick
:-(0)	shouting
:-)—	98-pound weakling
:-)	ha ha
:)	happy
:'-)	I am so happy, I am crying
:-)	I'm joking
-:-)	punk
:-)'	shall I get you a bib?
:-)	smiling
:)	smiling without a nose
:—————)	
	you are a big liar; Pinocchio
:-)*<|-)	happy Christmas
:):):)	loud guffaw
:)))	hugging that beer belly is like waking up holding a cold hot water bottle
:-)))	reeeaaaalllly happy
:-)))?	how many chins is it now?
:-)}	. . . and the goatee
:-)~	I am drooling (in anticipation)
:-)=	goofy; smiling with a beard
:-)8	smiling with bow tie; you look great
:-)K-	a shirt and tie at the gym – please?
:-*	bitter; bitter, moi?; kiss; ooops!
:-**	kisses

:*(	I am crying softly
:*(@)	you are drunk and shouting
:*)	I am drunk
:*)?	are you drunk?
:-/	I am sceptical
:/i	no smoking
::-(	four eyes
:-?	smoking a pipe
:-@	I am screaming
:@	it's true, I swear
:-@!	I am cursing
:@)	pig
:@))	you are a double chinned fat pig
:-@?	did you ever model for Picasso?
:@?	what?
:[	real downer
:-\	sceptical
:]	friendly; sarcasm is the lowest form of wit
:-]	you are very jolly; obnoxious
:-])	handlebar moustache
:^)	broken nose; I/you have a great personality; if you ain't pretty you better be nice
:^D	great! I like it!
:^U	forget it; I turn my face away
:^Y	I turn my poker face away
:-{)	with a moustache
:-{}	lipstick

:-{8	person who is unhappy with the results of their breast-enlargement surgery
:-|	have an ordinary day
:-|/:-I	no face/poker face
:-||	angry
:}	er?
:~-(	I am bawling
:~(	I'm feeling put out
:~(~~~	I am moved to tears
:-~)	having a cold
:+(	I am hurt by that remark
:-<	cheated
:-<>	surprised
:=)	two noses
:>	der?
:->	hey hey
:-£	I wouldn't say you were mean but you would rather swallow your cash than spend it
:-¥	shut up !
:-§(	call that a moustache?
:-0	ohhhhhh!
:-0WW	person vomiting a series of Slim Jims
:-6	sour, sure
:-7	that was a wry remark
:-8(	condescending stare
:8)	pig yourself
:-9	(mmm) I am licking my lips; salivating

:-C	I don't believe it!; I am really bummed
:C	liar
:-c	unhappy
:-D	I am very happy for you; laughter; yes, I am laughing at you
:D	laughter; yes, I'm laughing at you
:-e	I am disappointed
:-F	you are a bucktoothed vampire with one tooth missing
:I	hmmm ...
:-I	hmmm ...
:-I?	so?
:-J	tongue-in-cheek
:k	biting my lip
:-o	appalled; oh, no!; uh oh!
:-O	oops!; wow!
:O	yelling
:-o zz	bored
:-o zzzzZZ	I am bored, bored,bored
:-P	nyahhhh!
:-p——O	drool into a puddle
:-Q	smoking
:-S	I am confused; make sense; my last message didn't make sense
:-T	I am keeping a straight face
:-t	it's no good looking cross and pouting
:V	shouting

:-v	talking
:V:-|	person who cannot figure out why nobody wants to talk to him/her, little suspecting that there is an alligator on his/her head
:-W	liar (forked tongue); talking with two tongues
:-X	a big wet kiss; I am cross with you; my lips are sealed; not saying a word
:-X-	smoke no evil
:-Z	yes, I'm cross
;-)	twinkle
;)	twinkle (without nose); winking happy face, smirking
;-)	winking happy face; wink, wink, nudge, nudge
;?	wry remark, tongue in cheek
;}	leer
;->	winking happy face
?	what?/question(ing)
?!!	showing incredulity
?:)	one hair combed over makes no difference, you are still bald
?	why not?
@*&$!%	you know what that means . . .
@:-)	wearing a turban
@:)	wearing a turban without nose
@:-}	great new hairstyle!

@}—\———,—
       a rose
  @>—;— rose
  @>->— rose
@>—>— rose
       [:-) smiling with Walkman
       [:| Cyberman
        \ (profile) frowning
   \o/PTL praise the Lord; pass the loot
     ]:-> Satan's spawn
      ^ ^ happiness (Japanese symbol)
     ^L^ happy
      ^o snoring
      _! that's enough
      _. I am properly chastised and/or chagrined
_/~`·'~_/ I don't follow your line of thought
     _0-) scuba diver
   {(:-) no one loves a man with a bad toupee
    {:-) smiling with hair; toupee
  {:-()} great new hairstyle, moustache and beard
      {} 'no comment'
      |:) monobrow (missing link)
      |-) hee hee
      |* kiss (eyes closed)
     |:-| stubborn
     |:-0 big ohhhhhh!; no explanation given
     |-{ 'Good grief!' (Charlie Brown?)

|-D	ho ho
|-I	I am going to sleep; sleeping
|I	I am going to sleep; sleeping; of course you are not boring
|-0	I am bored; snoring
|P	yuk
}:-(	toupee blowing in the wind
};->	you are a rude devil
~:-(	steaming mad
~)	yummee
~0-(-D<	a baby
+!	yes
+!+!+!	YES! YES! YES!
+!!	very much so
+-)	I am cross-eyed
+<#^v	can I be your knight in shining armour? (profile)
+veD8n	positive dating
<&-I	I feel foolish and tearful
<)	drip
<:-(	dunce
<:)	was sad, now happy
<:-/	pointy head
<:-|	a monk or a nun
<:-0	eeek!
<^0^>	laugh loudly
<|-)	someone Chinese

```
         <=\   I am slightly offended
        <=-0   I am frightened
          <3   heart
        <3<3   a Time Lord (has two hearts)
         <G>   grinning
         <J>   joking
         <L>   laughing
         <O>   shouting
         <S>   smiling
          <X   a big wet kiss
         <X>   kissing
         <Y>   yawning
          -=   a doused candle to end a flame
           =   equal(s)
      -=#:-)   wizard
        =:-)   lose the moustache, lady
         =^)   I am/you are (so) open-minded
    =^..^=     miaow
     =|:-)=    Uncle Sam
       =-<>    I am awe-struck
===:[00']>:===
               I have been railroaded
        =-0    I am surprised; you do surprise me
       >:-(    very angry
       >:-)    devilish remarks
        >:)    little devil
       >:-<    sure I'm mad
```

>:-pq-:	two people pulling
>;-('	er! dumb or what?
>-<	absolutely livid
>>:)	feeling horny
>-> <)))">	fish
>-> <)))">&{{{{{{	fish and crinkle-cut chips
>-> <)))"D>&|||||||||||||	fish and chips
>8>-(-<	Woody the Woodpecker
>-COD	I am 'floundering' for something to say
>w	oh really! (ironic)
£$:-))) GOdLuK	you are a money magnet (good luck getting that pay rise)
££$$CumsEsilE2YaHnds	money comes easily to your hands
§:-)	I have curly hair
§;-(	you are behaving like a lawyer
§; ^ ()	the law is an ass
0*-)	angel winking
3:-)	butt head
3:~v	butt head
3:-o	silly moo
4/> <: -})	you are behaving like an estate agent
404	file not found
7= ^ >	I am happy (three-quarter view)
8-)	smiling with glasses

8:-)	glasses on head
8:]	gorilla
80!	oh, my God!
8-S	sees all evil
B-)	sunglasses
B:)	bisexual
B:-)	sunglasses on head
C:-)	large brain – no ideas
C|:-)	smiling with top hat
d :-)	hats off to your great idea
d:-)	smiling with cap
G:)-	gay man
G:)	glad to be gay
i-=<*** __.CAUTION:	
	has flame thrower and uses it!
i-=<****** o-(==<CAUTION:	
	has flame thrower and uses it!
i-=<***iCAUTION:	
	has flame thrower
I8*I	the devil; a cat
IGA!¬(	I've got a black eye
L:-)	congratulations on your graduation
L:)	lesbian
M:-)	I salute you (respect)
M:-) Yaslf	respect yourself
o'!	I am feeling pretty grim (profile)
o'"	I am pursing my lips (profile)

0-(==<	I am chastised and/or chagrined
0:-)	an angel (with a halo); for those innocent souls
ø;^)	do you come from another planet?
o'	frowning (profile)
o'P	I stick my tongue out at you (profile)
o=	a burning candle for flames (shouting messages of an unpleasant nature)
0-G-<	me, me, me, that's all you ever think about
o'J	smiling (profile)
00	please read now (headlights on message)
o'r	sticking tongue out (profile)
0-S-<	I'm outta here
o'T	keeping a straight face (profile)
o'U	yawning (profile)
o'V	shouting (profile)
o'v	talking (profile)
o'w	lying(profile)
o'Y	whistling (profile)
'P	(profile) sticking tongue out
P-)	got a black eye; nudge, nudge, wink, wink
Q:)	queer
r:-)	mmm, ponytail spells loser
s:-)i—<	weird-hair guy/gal
'T	keeping a straight face (profile)
'U	yawning (profile)
U*8=(:	you blithering idiot

'V	shouting (profile)
'v	talking (profile)
X	kiss
X-(	you are mad
X:-"	ex-heavy smoker
X:-Q	ex-smoker
X:UjX	you can't smoke and smile at the same time
Xoxoxoxo	hugs and kisses
'Y	whistling (profile)